Coaching Youth Track & Field

American Sport Education Program

Official Handbook of Hershey's Track & Field Games

Endorsed by the USATF

Human Kinetics

Library of Congress Cataloging-in-Publication Data

Coaching youth track & field / American Sport Education Program.
    p. cm.
  ISBN-13: 978-0-7360-6914-4 (soft cover)
  ISBN-10: 0-7360-6914-3 (soft cover)
  1. Track and field for children--Coaching. I. American Sport
Education Program. II. Title: Coaching youth track and field.
  GV1060.9.C63 2008
  796.42083--dc22
                            2007038400

ISBN: 978-0-7360-6914-4

The Web addresses cited in this text were current as of October 2007, unless otherwise noted.

Acquisitions Editors: Emma Sandberg and Jenny Maddox; **Project Writer:** Matt Lydum; **Developmental Editor:** Laura Floch; **Assistant Editor:** Cory Weber; **Copyeditor:** Pat Connolly; **Proofreader:** Bethany J. Bentley; **Permission Manager:** Carly Breeding; **Graphic Designer:** Nancy Rasmus; **Graphic Artist:** Kim McFarland; **Cover Designer:** Keith Blomberg; **Photographer (cover):** Paul McMahon; **Photographer (interior):** Neil Bernstein; photos on pages 1, 11, 21, 33, 45, 49, 55, 67, 99, 113, 143, 177, 187, and 201 © Human Kinetics; **Photo Asset Manager:** Laura Fitch; **Visual Production Assistant:** Joyce Brumfield; **Photo Office Assistant:** Jason Allen; **Art Manager:** Kelly Hendren; **Associate Art Manager:** Alan L. Wilborn; **Illustrator:** Lineworks, Inc.; **Printer:** Total Printing Systems

We thank Mahomet High School in Mahomet, Illinois, for assistance in providing the location for the photo shoot for this book.

Copies of this book are available at special discounts for bulk purchase for sales promotions, premiums, fund-raising, or educational use. Special editions or book excerpts can also be created to specifications. For details, contact the Special Sales Manager at Human Kinetics.

Printed in the United States of America   20 19 18 17 16 15 14 13 12

The paper in this book is certified under a sustainable forestry program.

Human Kinetics
1607 N. Market Street
Champaign, IL 61820
USA

United States and International
Website: **US.HumanKinetics.com**
Email: info@hkusa.com
Phone: 1-800-747-4457

Canada
Website: **Canada.HumanKinetics.com**
Email: info@hkcanada.com

Tell us what you think!
Human Kinetics would love to hear what we can do to improve the customer experience. Use this QR code to take our brief survey.

Contents

Welcome to Coaching

Coaching young people is an exciting way to be involved in sport. But it isn't easy. Some coaches are overwhelmed by the responsibilities involved in helping athletes through their early sport experiences. And that's not surprising because coaching youngsters can require you to do everything from standing at the finish line with a stopwatch to unlocking the equipment shed. It also involves preparing them physically and mentally to compete effectively, fairly, and safely in their sport and providing them with a positive role model.

Coaching Youth Track & Field will help you meet the challenges and experience the many rewards of coaching young athletes. You'll learn how to meet your responsibilities as a coach, communicate well, provide for safety, and teach skills while keeping them fun. Plus, you'll learn strategies for coaching competitions. You will find many activities specifically oriented toward coaching children in the sport of track and field included throughout the text to help you with your practices. We also provide a sample practice plan and season plan to guide you throughout your season.

For more information about this product or other American Sport Education Program resources, please contact us:

ASEP
P.O. Box 5076
Champaign, IL 61825-5076
800-747-5698
www.ASEP.com

Welcome From Hershey's and USATF

On behalf of Hershey's and USATF, welcome to *Coaching Youth Track & Field*. It is one of many resources available to you through the American Sport Education Program (ASEP), Hershey's Track & Field Games, and USA Track & Field (USATF). Whether it's learning how to teach proper fundamental skills or how to communicate better, this book can guide you through your experience of coaching youth track and field.

You will find this book easy to follow and an excellent introduction to youth coaching with fresh ideas on how to coach children in the sport of track and field. These methods may be very different from the way you were coached, but they are best for developing and mentoring passionate athletes who can, in turn, pass their knowledge on to younger kids and help expose them to the sport. This book contains information on how to coach a successful team starting with the first day of practice to the final meet of the season, while along the way teaching young athletes valuable skills. Also included are fun activities and plenty of resources to aid you in your coaching journey.

In working with the American Sport Education Program (ASEP), our goal is to provide youth coaches with effective resources to help expand their knowledge of the sport and ensure that every coach and every athlete has a positive experience. For you, the benefits of coaching last a lifetime; your coaching will have a profound effect on the many athletes you influence—not just for today, but for many years to come.

Thank you for coaching youth track and field!

Stepping Into Coaching

I f you are like most youth sport coaches, you have probably been recruited from the ranks of concerned parents, sport enthusiasts, or community volunteers. Like many rookie and veteran coaches, you probably have had little formal instruction on how to coach. But when the call went out for coaches to assist with the local youth track and field program, you answered because you like children and enjoy track and field, and perhaps because you wanted to be involved in a worthwhile community activity.

Your initial coaching assignment may be difficult. Like many volunteers, you may not know everything there is to know about track and field or about how to work with children. *Coaching Youth Track & Field* presents the basics of coaching track and field effectively. To start, we look at your responsibilities and what's involved in being a coach. We also talk about what to do when your own child is on the team you coach, and we examine five tools for being an effective coach.

Your Responsibilities as a Coach

Coaching at any level involves much more than choosing the relay team or teaching your athletes how to use the starting blocks. Coaching involves accepting the tremendous responsibility you face when parents put their children in your care. As a track and field coach, you'll be called on to do the following:

1. *Provide a safe physical environment.*

   Participating in track and field holds inherent risks, but as a coach you're responsible for regularly inspecting the areas and equipment used for practice and competition (see "Facilities and Equipment Checklist" in appendix A on page 210). You should reassure athletes and parents that you will be teaching the safest techniques in order to help athletes avoid injury and that you have an emergency action plan in place (see chapter 4 for more information).

2. *Communicate in a positive way.*

   As you already know, you have a lot to communicate. You'll communicate not only with your athletes and their parents, but also with the coaching staff, officials, administrators, and others. Communicate in a positive way that demonstrates that you have the best interests of the athletes at heart (see chapter 2 for more information).

3. *Teach the fundamental skills of track and field.*

   When teaching the fundamental skills of track and field, keep in mind that you always want to be sure that your athletes have fun. Therefore, we ask that you help all athletes be the best they can be by creating a fun yet productive practice environment. To help you do this, we'll show you an innovative games approach to teaching and practicing the skills young athletes need to know—an approach that kids thoroughly enjoy (see chapter 5 for more information). Additionally, to help your athletes improve their skills, you need to have a sound understanding of track and field skills (the information in chapters 7 through 11 will help you gain that understanding).

4. *Teach the rules of track and field.*

Introduce the rules of track and field, and incorporate them into individual instruction (see chapter 3 for more information). Many rules can be taught in practice, including lane guidelines, start commands, field event rules, and general track and field etiquette. Plan to review the rules any time an opportunity naturally arises in practices.

5. *Direct athletes in competition.*

Your responsibilities include determining meet entries, relating appropriately to officials and to opposing coaches and athletes, and making sound decisions during meets (see chapter 12 for more information on coaching during meets). Remember that the focus is not on winning at all costs but on coaching your kids to compete well, do their best, improve their track and field skills, and strive to win within the rules.

6. *Help your athletes to become fit and to value fitness for a lifetime.*

We want you to help your athletes be fit so they can participate in track and field safely and successfully. We also want your athletes to learn to become fit on their own, understand the value of fitness, and enjoy training. Thus, we ask you not to make them do push-ups or run laps for punishment. Make it fun to get fit, and make it fun to participate in track and field so that your athletes will stay fit for a lifetime.

7. *Help young people develop character.*

Character development includes learning, caring, being honest and respectful, and taking responsibility. These intangible qualities are no less important to teach than the skill of long jumping. We ask you to teach these values to athletes by demonstrating and encouraging behaviors that express these values at all times. For example, stress to young athletes the importance of encouraging their teammates, competing within the rules, and showing respect for their opponents.

These are your responsibilities as a coach. Remember that every athlete is an individual. You must provide a wholesome environment in which every athlete has the opportunity to learn without fear while having fun and enjoying the overall track and field experience.

Coaching Paralympic Track and Field

One of the great advantages of the sport of track and field is that all children can participate. Children with disabilities have great opportunities to become involved in Paralympic competition.

In Paralympic track and field, athletes compete in track and field events grouped according to common disabilities. The major classification groups are blind and visually impaired athletes, who compete in the track events and field events; athletes with cerebral palsy and traumatic brain injury, who also compete in both track and field events; athletes with dwarfism, who compete in the throwing events only (shot and discus); amputees, where there are classes for both-arm amputees and above- and below-the-knee amputees in track and field; and wheelchair athletes, who compete in both track races and throwing events from a throwing chair. Athletes in these classifications are grouped according to level of function so that athletes of similar levels of disability compete on an even playing field.

Sadly, many children with disabilities will not reach their potential as athletes because of lack of coaching. Roughly half of our national-class Paralympic track and field athletes (including several medal winners at the highest levels of competition) are either undercoached (by a well-intentioned "coach" without even a basic knowledge of sport science, training theory, or event coaching) or completely uncoached. That does not address the hundreds of potential athletes in the United States who never even begin to participate in our sport because a coach thought, *There's no way I could coach an athlete with a physical disability. I wouldn't know where to start.* In reality, however, there are many more similarities in coaching these athletes than there are differences. The basics of technique and training are the same. With a little experience, many coaches would realize that they could train Paralympic athletes.

If you know of athletes who might be eligible for Paralympic competitions, or if you would like further information on coaching Paralympic track and field athletes, please contact the United States Olympic Committee or visit www.usoc.org.

Coaching Your Own Child

Coaching can become even more complicated when your child is on the team you coach. Many coaches are parents, but the two roles should not be confused. As a parent, you are responsible only for yourself and your child, but as a coach you are also responsible for the organization, all the athletes on the team, and their parents. Because of this additional responsibility, your

Coaching Tip

Be sure to discuss your interest in coaching track and field with your child before making a decision. If your child has strong reservations about you taking the job of head coach, you should consider becoming involved in a smaller role instead. For example, you can be an assistant coach, serve as the statistician for the team, or organize a group of parents who provide drinks and snacks at practices and competitions.

behavior as a coach will be different from your behavior at home, and your son or daughter may not understand why.

For example, imagine the confusion of a young boy who is the center of his parents' attention at home but is barely noticed by his father (who is the coach) in the sport setting. Or consider the mixed signals received by a young girl whose skill is constantly evaluated by a coach (who is also her mother) who otherwise rarely comments on her daughter's activities. You need to explain to your child your new responsibilities and how they will affect your relationship when coaching. Take the following steps to avoid problems when coaching your own child:

- Ask your child if he wants you to coach the team.
- Explain why you want to be involved with the team.
- Discuss with your child how your interactions will change when you take on the role of coach at practices or competitions.
- Limit your coaching behavior to when you are in the coaching role.
- Avoid parenting during practice or competitions to keep your role clear in your child's mind.
- Reaffirm your love for your child, irrespective of his performance.

Five Tools of an Effective Coach

Have you purchased the traditional coaching tools—such as a stopwatch, a tape measure, coaching clothes, and a clipboard? They'll help you in the act of coaching, but to be successful, you'll need five other tools that cannot be bought. These tools are available only through self-examination and hard work; they're easy to remember with the acronym COACH:

C   Comprehension

O   Outlook

A   Affection

C   Character

H   Humor

Comprehension

Comprehension of the rules and skills of track and field is required. You must understand the basic elements of the sport. To improve your comprehension of track and field, take the following steps:

- Read about the rules of track and field in chapter 3 of this book.
- Read about the fundamental skills of track and field in chapters 7 through 11.
- Read additional track and field coaching books, including those available from the American Sport Education Program (ASEP) and Human Kinetics.
- Contact youth track and field organizations such as Hershey's Track & Field Games (www.hersheystrackandfield.com) and USA Track & Field (www.usatf.org).
- Attend track and field coaching clinics.
- Talk with more experienced coaches.
- Observe local college, high school, and youth track and field events.
- Watch track and field events on television.

Coaching Tip

Attending local college and high school track and field events is a low-cost way not only for you to improve your knowledge of the sport, but also for athletes of all ages to observe the skills of track and field. Consider working with your team's parents to organize a team outing to a local event in place of an after-school or weekend practice.

In addition to having track and field knowledge, you must implement proper training and safety methods so that your athletes can participate with little risk of injury. Even then, injuries may occur. And more often than not, you'll be the first person responding to your athletes' injuries, so be sure you understand the basic emergency care procedures described in chapter 4. Also, read in that chapter how to handle more serious sport injury situations.

Outlook

The second coaching tool refers to your perspective and goals—what you seek as a coach. The most common coaching objectives are to have fun; to help athletes develop their physical, mental, and social skills; and to strive to win. Thus, your outlook involves your priorities, your planning, and your vision for the future. See "Assessing Your Priorities" to learn more about the priorities you set for yourself as a coach.

Assessing Your Priorities

Even though all coaches focus on competition, we want you to focus on *positive* competition—keeping the pursuit of victory in perspective by making decisions that, first, are in the best interest of the athletes and, second, will help them to succeed.

So, how do you know if your outlook and priorities are in order? Here's a little test:

1. Which situation would you be most proud of?
   a. *knowing that each participant enjoyed participating in track and field*
   b. *seeing that all athletes improved their track and field skills*
   c. *watching your athletes win championships*

2. Which statement best reflects your thoughts about sport?
   a. *If it isn't fun, don't do it.*
   b. *Everyone should learn something every day.*
   c. *Sport isn't fun if you don't win.*

3. How would you like your athletes to remember you?
   a. *as a coach who was fun*
   b. *as a coach who provided a good base of fundamental skills*
   c. *as a coach who helped them to win*

4. Which would you most like to hear a parent of an athlete on your team say?
   a. *Nicole really had a good time participating in track and field this year.*
   b. *Josh learned some important lessons participating in track and field this year.*
   c. *Megan won every track and field throwing event this year.*

5. Which of the following would be the most rewarding moment of your season?
   a. *having your team want to continue practicing, even after practice is over*
   b. *seeing one of your athletes finally master her approach on the long jump*
   c. *watching one of your athletes qualify for the national meet*

Look over your answers. If you most often selected "a" responses, then having fun is most important to you. A majority of "b" answers suggests that skill development is what attracts you to coaching. And if "c" was your most frequent response, winning is tops on your list of coaching priorities. If your priorities are in order, your athletes' well-being will take precedence over your team's success every time.

ASEP has a motto that will help you keep your outlook in line with the best interests of the kids on your team. It summarizes in four words all you need to remember when establishing your coaching priorities:

Athletes First, Winning Second

This motto recognizes that striving to win is an important, even vital, part of sports. But it emphatically states that no efforts in striving to win should be made at the expense of the athletes' well-being, development, and enjoyment. Take the following actions to better define your outlook:

- With the members of your coaching staff, determine your priorities for the season.
- Prepare for situations that may challenge your priorities.
- Set goals for yourself and your athletes that are consistent with your priorities.
- Plan how you and your athletes can best attain your goals.
- Review your goals frequently to be sure that you are staying on track.

Affection

Another vital tool you will want to have in your coaching kit is a genuine concern for the young people you coach. This requires having a passion for kids, a desire to share with them your enjoyment and knowledge of track and field, and the patience and understanding that allow all your athletes to grow from their involvement in sport. You can demonstrate your affection and patience in many ways, including the following:

- Make an effort to get to know each athlete on your team.
- Treat each athlete as an individual.
- Empathize with athletes trying to learn new and difficult skills.
- Treat athletes as you would like to be treated under similar circumstances.
- Control your emotions.
- Show your enthusiasm for being involved with your team.
- Keep an upbeat tempo and a positive tone in all your communications.

Character

The fact that you have decided to coach young track and field athletes probably means that you think participation in sport is important. But whether or not that participation develops character in your athletes depends as much on you as it does on the sport itself. How can you help your athletes build character?

To teach kids good character, coaches must model appropriate behaviors for sport and life. That means more than just saying the right things. What you say and what you do must match. There is no place in coaching for the "Do as I say, not as I do" philosophy. Challenge, support, encourage, and reward every youngster, and your athletes will be more likely to accept, even celebrate, their differences. Be in control before, during, and after all practices and competitions. And don't be afraid to admit that you were wrong. No one is perfect!

Each member of your coaching staff should consider the following steps to becoming a good role model:

- Take stock of your strengths and weaknesses.
- Build on your strengths.
- Set goals for yourself to improve on those areas that you don't want to see copied.
- If you slip up, apologize to your team and to yourself. You'll do better next time.

Humor

Humor is an often overlooked coaching tool. It means having the ability to laugh at yourself and with your athletes during practices and competitions. Nothing helps balance the seriousness of a skill session like a chuckle or two. And a sense of humor puts in perspective the many mistakes your athletes will make. So don't get upset over each dropped baton or respond negatively to fouls. Allow yourself and your athletes to enjoy the ups, and don't dwell on the downs. Here are some tips for injecting humor and fun into your practices:

- Make practices fun by including a variety of activities.
- Keep all athletes involved during practice.
- Consider laughter by your athletes to be a sign of enjoyment, not of waning discipline.
- Smile!

Communicating
as a Coach

I n chapter 1, you learned about the tools you need for coaching: comprehension, outlook, affection, character, and humor. These are essentials for effective coaching; without them, you'd have a difficult time getting started. But none of the tools will work if you don't know how to use them with your athletes—and this requires skillful communication. This chapter examines what communication is and how you can become a more effective communicator.

Coaches often mistakenly believe that communication occurs only when instructing athletes to do something, but verbal commands are only a small part of the communication process. More than half of the communication between people is nonverbal. So when you are coaching, remember that actions speak louder than words.

Communication in its simplest form involves two people: a sender and a receiver. The sender transmits the message verbally, through facial expressions, and possibly through body language. Once the message is sent, the receiver must receive it and, optimally, understand it. A receiver who fails to pay attention or listen will miss part, if not all, of the message.

Sending Effective Messages

Young athletes often have little understanding of the rules and skills of track and field and probably even less confidence in their ability to perform. So they need accurate, understandable, and supportive messages to help them along. That's why your verbal and nonverbal messages are important.

Verbal Messages

"Sticks and stones may break my bones, but words will never hurt me" isn't true. Spoken words can have a strong and long-lasting effect. And coaches' words are particularly influential because youngsters place great importance on what coaches say. Perhaps you, like many former youth sport participants, have a difficult time remembering much of anything your elementary school teachers told you, but you can probably still recall several specific things your coaches at that level said. Such is the lasting effect of a coach's comments to an athlete.

Whether you are correcting misbehavior, teaching a sprinter correct starting techniques, or praising a thrower for good effort, you should consider a number of things when sending a message verbally:

- Be positive and honest.
- Speak clearly and simply.
- Say it loud enough, then say it again.
- Be consistent.

Be Positive and Honest

Nothing turns people off like hearing someone nag all the time, and athletes react similarly to a coach who gripes constantly. Kids particularly need encouragement because they often doubt their ability to perform in a sport. So look for and tell your athletes what they did well.

But don't cover up poor or incorrect technique with rosy words of praise. Kids know all too well when they've erred, and no cheerfully expressed cliche can undo their mistakes. If you fail to acknowledge errors, your athletes will think you are a phony.

An effective way to correct a performance error is to first point out the part of the skill that the athlete performed correctly. Then explain—in a positive manner—the error that the athlete made, and show her the correct way to do it. Finish by encouraging the athlete and emphasizing the correct performance.

Make sure you don't follow a positive statement with the word *but*. For example, you shouldn't say, "Way to hit your mark, Kelly, but if you drive your knee next time, you'll be able to jump much farther." Many kids will ignore the positive statement and focus on the negative one. Instead, you could say, "That was a good approach on the runway, Kelly. And if you focus on driving your knee up, you'll be able to hit a really big jump. Way to go."

Speak Clearly and Simply

Positive and honest messages are most effective when expressed directly in words your athletes understand. Beating around the bush is ineffective and inefficient. And if you ramble, your athletes will miss the point of your message and probably lose interest. Here are some tips for saying things clearly:

- Organize your thoughts before speaking to your athletes.
- Know your subject as completely as possible.
- Explain things thoroughly, but don't bore your athletes with long-winded monologues.
- Use language your athletes can understand, and be consistent in your terminology. However, avoid trying to be hip by using their age group's slang.

Say It Loud Enough, Then Say It Again

Talk to your team in a voice that all members can hear. A crisp, vigorous voice commands attention and respect; garbled and weak speech is tuned out. It's okay and, in fact, appropriate to soften your voice when speaking to an athlete individually about a personal problem. But most of the time your messages will be for all your athletes to hear, so make sure they can! An enthusiastic voice also motivates athletes and tells them you enjoy being their coach. A word of caution, however: Avoid dominating the setting with a booming voice that distracts attention from athletes' performances.

Coaching Tip

Remember, terms that you are familiar with and understand may be completely foreign to your athletes, especially younger athletes or beginners. Adjust your vocabulary to match the age group. Although 12- to 14-year-olds may understand terms such as "false start" or "nonvisual exchange," 8- and 9-year-olds may be confused by this terminology. In some cases, you may need to use demonstrations with the athletes so they can "see" the term and how it relates to track and field.

Sometimes what you say, even if stated loudly and clearly, won't sink in the first time. This may be particularly true when young athletes hear words they don't understand. To avoid boring repetition and still get your message across, you can say the same thing in a slightly different way. For instance, when explaining a drill, you might first tell your athletes, "Use your arms!" If the athletes don't appear to understand, you might say, "Running arms!" The second form of the message may get through to athletes who missed it the first time around.

Be Consistent

People often say things in ways that imply a different message. For example, a touch of sarcasm added to "Way to go!" sends an entirely different message than the words themselves suggest. You should avoid sending mixed messages. Keep the tone of your voice consistent with the words you use. And don't say something one day and contradict it the next; athletes will get their wires crossed.

You also want to keep your terminology consistent. Many track and field terms describe the same or similar skills. Take one popular warm-up drill, for example. One coach may use the term "grapevine" to refer to this move, while another coach may say "carioca." Although both might be correct, to be consistent as a staff, the coaches of a team should agree on all terms before the start of the season and then stay with them.

Nonverbal Messages

Just as you should be consistent in the tone of voice and words you use, you should also keep your verbal and nonverbal messages consistent. An extreme example of failing to do this is shaking your head, indicating disapproval, while at the same time telling an athlete, "Nice try." Which is the athlete to believe, your gesture or your words?

Messages can be sent nonverbally in several ways. Facial expressions and body language are just two of the more obvious forms of nonverbal signals that can help you when you coach. Keep in mind that as a coach you need to be a teacher first, and any action that detracts from the message you are trying to convey should be avoided.

Facial Expressions

The look on a person's face is the quickest clue to what the person thinks. Your athletes know this, so they will study your face, looking for a sign that will tell them more than the words you say. Don't try to fool them by putting on a happy or blank "mask." They'll see through it, and you'll lose credibility.

Serious, stone-faced expressions provide no cues to kids who want to know how they are performing. When faced with this, kids will just assume you're unhappy or disinterested. Don't be afraid to smile. A smile from a coach can give a great boost to an unsure athlete. Plus, a smile lets your athletes know you are happy coaching them. But don't overdo it, or your athletes won't be able to tell when you are genuinely pleased by something they've done or when you are just putting on a smiling face.

Body Language

What would your athletes think you were feeling if you came to practice slouched over, with your head down and your shoulders slumped? Would they think you were tired, bored, or unhappy? What would they think you were feeling if you watched them during a competition with your hands on your hips, your jaws clenched, and your face reddened? Would they think you were upset with them, disgusted at an official, or mad at a fan? Probably some or all of these things would enter your athletes' minds. And none is the impression you want your athletes to have of you. That's why you should carry yourself in a pleasant, confident, and vigorous manner.

Coaching Tip

As a coach, you need to be aware of your body language. Athletes of all ages will pick up on your actions and habits, so you must ensure that you provide a good example for your athletes to model. All it takes is a few eye rolls or wild hand gestures to send a message that this type of behavior is acceptable, even if that would never be your intent.

Physical contact can also be a very important use of body language. A high five, a pat on the head, an arm around the shoulder, and even a big hug are effective ways to show approval, concern, affection, and joy to your players. Youngsters are especially in need of this type of nonverbal message. Keep within the obvious moral and legal limits, of course, but don't be reluctant to touch your athletes, sending a message that can be expressed only in that way.

Improving Your Receiving Skills

Now let's examine the other half of the communication process: receiving messages. Too often very good senders are very poor receivers of messages. But as a coach of young athletes, you must be able to fulfill both roles effectively.

The requirements for receiving messages are simple, but receiving skills are perhaps less satisfying and therefore underdeveloped compared with sending skills. People seem to enjoy hearing themselves talk more than they enjoy hearing others talk. But if you learn the keys to receiving messages and make a strong effort to use them with your athletes, you'll be surprised by what you've been missing.

Pay Attention

First, you must pay attention; you must want to hear what others need to communicate to you. That's not always easy when you're busy coaching and have many things competing for your attention. But in one-on-one or team meetings with athletes, you must focus on what they are telling you, both verbally and nonverbally. You'll be amazed at the little signals you pick up. This focused attention will not only help you catch every word your athletes say, but it will also enable you to notice your athletes' moods and physical states. In addition, you'll get an idea of your athletes' feelings toward you and other athletes on the team.

Listen Carefully

How you receive messages from others, perhaps more than anything else you do, demonstrates how much you care for the sender and what that person has to tell you. If you care little for your athletes or have little regard for what they have to say, it will show in how you attend and listen to them. You need to check yourself. Do you find your mind wandering to what you are going to do after practice while one of your athletes is talking to you? Do you frequently have to ask your athletes, "What did you say?" If so, you need to work on your receiving mechanics of attending and listening. But if you find that you're missing the messages your athletes send, perhaps the most critical question you should ask yourself is this: "Do I care enough to be a coach?"

Providing Feedback

So far we've discussed separately the sending and receiving of messages. But we all know that senders and receivers switch roles several times during an interaction. One person initiates a communication by sending a message to another person, who then receives the message. The receiver then becomes the sender by responding to the person who sent the initial message. These verbal and nonverbal responses are called *feedback*.

Your athletes will look to you for feedback all the time. They will want to know how you think they are performing, what you think of their ideas, and whether their efforts please you. You can respond in many different ways, and how you respond will strongly affect your athletes. They will react most favorably to positive feedback.

Praising athletes when they have performed or behaved well is an effective way to get them to repeat (or try to repeat) that behavior. And positive feedback for effort is an especially effective way to motivate youngsters to work on difficult skills. So rather than shouting at and providing negative feedback to athletes who have made mistakes, you should try offering positive feedback and letting them know what they did correctly and how they can improve.

Sometimes just the way you word feedback can make it more positive than negative. For example, instead of saying, "Don't go out too hard," you might say, "Go out at a smart, comfortable pace." Then your athletes will be focusing on what to do instead of what not to do.

Positive feedback can be verbal or nonverbal. Telling young athletes, especially in front of teammates, that they have performed well is a great way to boost their confidence. And a pat on the back or a high five communicates that you recognize an athlete's performance.

Communicating With Other Groups

In addition to sending and receiving messages and providing proper feedback to athletes, coaching also involves interacting with members of the coaching staff, parents, fans, officials, and opposing coaches. If you don't communicate effectively with these groups, your coaching career will be unpleasant and short lived. So try the following suggestions for communicating with these groups.

Coaching Staff

Before you hold your first practice, the coaching staff should meet and discuss the roles and responsibilities that each coach will undertake during the year. Depending on the number of assistant coaches, the staff responsibilities can be divided into different areas. For example, one coach may be in charge of working with the jumpers, while another is responsible for teaching the throws. The head coach has the final responsibility for the team, but as much as possible, the assistant coaches should be responsible for their areas.

Before practices start, the coaching staff must also discuss and agree on terminology, plans for practices, meet day organization, the method of communicating during practices and competitions, and event conditions. The coaches on your staff must present a united front and speak with one voice, and they must all take a similar approach to coaching, interacting with the athletes and parents, and interacting with one another. Disagreements should be discussed away from the track, and each coach should have a say as the staff comes to an agreement.

Coaching Tip

Although all the coaches on your staff need to share similar coaching philosophies and be able to work together, you and your assistant coaches don't have to be identical. On the contrary, you should look for assistant coaches who can complement areas where you aren't as strong. For example, perhaps you're confident in your ability to teach the fundamentals of running, but you're not very familiar with the nuances of hurdling. In this situation, you could consider recruiting assistant coaches who can take over some of the responsibilities in that area.

Parents

An athlete's parents need to be assured that their son or daughter is under the direction of a coach who is both knowledgeable about the sport and concerned about the youngster's well-being. You can put their worries to rest by holding a preseason parent orientation meeting in which you describe your background and your approach to coaching. See "Preseason Meeting Topics" for a sample outline of information to cover at a parent orientation meeting. (Note that the type of paperwork needed before the season starts, as well as the procedures and costs for handing out or purchasing equipment, will vary by team.)

Preseason Meeting Topics

1. Share your coaching philosophy.
2. Outline the paperwork that is needed:
   - Copy of the athlete's birth certificate
   - Completed athlete's application and payment record
   - Report card from the previous year
   - Participation agreement form
   - Informed consent form
   - Emergency information card
3. Go over the inherent risks of track and field and other safety issues. Review your emergency action plan.
4. Inform parents of procedures related to uniforms and equipment, including what items the team will provide and what equipment the athletes must furnish themselves.
5. Review the season practice schedule, including the date, location, and time of each practice.
6. Go over the proper gear and attire that should be worn at each practice session.
7. Discuss nutrition, hydration, and rest for athletes.
8. Explain the goals for the team.
9. Cover methods of communication: e-mail list, emergency phone numbers, interactive Web site, and so on.
10. Discuss ways that parents can help with the team.
11. Discuss standards of conduct for coaches, athletes, and parents.
12. Provide time for questions and answers.

If parents contact you with a concern during the season, you should listen to them closely and try to offer positive responses. If you need to communicate with parents, you can catch them after a practice or meet, give them a phone call, or send a note through e-mail or regular mail. Messages sent to parents through athletes are too often lost, misinterpreted, or forgotten.

Fans

The stands probably won't be overflowing at your competitions, which means that you'll more easily hear the few fans who criticize your coaching. When you hear something negative about the job you're doing, don't respond. Keep calm, consider whether the message had any value, and if not, forget it. Acknowledging critical, unwarranted comments from a fan during a meet will only encourage others to voice their opinions. So put away your "rabbit ears" and communicate to fans, through your actions, that you are a confident, competent coach.

You must also prepare your athletes for fans' criticisms. Tell your athletes that it is you, not the spectators, that they should listen to. If you notice that one of your athletes is rattled by a fan's comment, you should reassure the athlete that your evaluation is more objective and favorable—and the one that counts.

Officials

How you communicate with officials will have a great influence on the way your athletes behave toward them. Therefore, you must set a good example. Greet officials with a handshake, an introduction, and perhaps casual conversation about the upcoming competition. Indicate your respect for them before, during, and after the events. Don't shout, make nasty remarks, or use disrespectful body gestures. Your athletes will see your actions and get the idea that such behavior is appropriate. Plus, if the official hears or sees you, the communication between the two of you will break down.

Opposing Coaches

Make an effort to visit with the coach of the opposing teams before the competition. During the meet, don't get into a personal feud with another coach. Remember, it's the kids, not the coaches, who are competing. And by getting along well with the opposing coaches, you'll show your players that competition involves cooperation.

3

Understanding Rules and Equipment

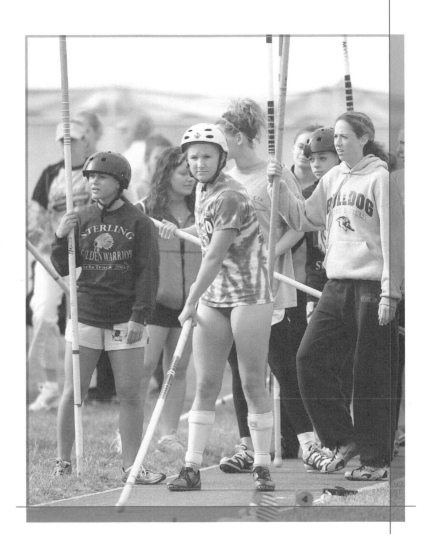

The objectives of track and field are simple: run fast, jump far or high, and throw far. That said, the number of individual events in track and field can make things tough on new coaches who might feel overwhelmed at first. This introduction to the basic rules of track and field won't cover every rule of the sport but instead will tell you what you need to know to work with athletes who are 8 to 14 years old. In this chapter, we cover the basics of the sport, such as equipment, implement sizes, and meet procedures. We also describe specifics such as event etiquette and rules of competition, then we wrap things up with some officiating basics.

Age Modifications for Track and Field

Before we begin, let's consider some of the modifications that can be made to accommodate different age groups. Things such as race distances and implement sizes, along with some competition rules, can be adjusted for the various age groups to help accommodate athletes' development and skill levels. The following table outlines basic modifications (by age group) as recommended by Hershey's Track & Field Games and USA Track & Field (USATF). Local clubs and school programs are encouraged to follow or modify these rules as they deem appropriate for the ages and skill levels of the athletes.

Also note that many local clubs welcome athletes younger than the age ranges listed in the table, providing opportunities for athletes in the 8-and-under category, and even 6 and under. For these age groups, the emphasis is on teaching the basic skills of track and field, and there may or may not be organized competitions. At these younger levels, coaches commonly use modified activities to introduce the most basic concepts of running, jumping, and throwing.

Table 3.1   Age Modifications for Track and Field

	Beginners: ages 11 and under	Intermediate: ages 12 to 13	Advanced: ages 14 and over
Sprints	Park and recreation meets and outreach events often stage races for children on grass fields. This is an appropriate level of sprinting for this age group. At more organized meets, races that last more than 90 seconds (such as the 400-meter dash) are more like a middle-distance race. To help athletes develop skill in full-speed running, keep many training and racing distances short enough so that athletes can finish in less than 12 seconds.	Children at this developmental level usually compete using the adult program. Again, full-speed running can only be maintained for a short amount of time. So keep many training distances short. Also, you must be sure not to overrace young sprinters during this developmental time.	As children get into adolescence, many have developed enough body strength to coordinate their limbs as they approach full-speed running. Energy system training becomes more appropriate, and the level of competition (including state and national championships) becomes significantly more intense. Although athletes may seem physically mature, you should work carefully to ensure that they will benefit from the higher pressure of major championships.

	Beginners: ages 11 and under	Intermediate: ages 12 to 13	Advanced: ages 14 and over
Jumps	The running long jump is available at many meets for this age group. Also, the standing long jump is an appropriate event for young children. You can also provide children with early exposure to jumping skills through fun competitions such as the 10-meter speed hop and the scissors high jump.	Children at this level begin gaining the consistency to really compete in the running long jump. This is a good time to introduce the triple jump and other bounding activities. With proper coaching, some children could begin doing pole vault drills and mastering the back layout style of high jumping.	Early in adolescence, athletes begin competing in a program of jumping activities that mirrors the adult model: running long jump, triple jump, high jump (generally using the back layout style), and pole vault.
Throws	Young children often compete using the softball throw and minijavelin. Also, many opportunities are available for children to put the shot. Throwing activities with medicine balls are a good option for early exposure and training.	During this developmental period, competition that begins to look more like the adult model starts taking place. However, you should keep implements relatively light so that athletes can learn technique and speed as their strength levels improve.	In junior high school, boys generally throw slightly smaller implements. Typically, however, girls begin throwing the high school and college implements at this time. For the USATF Junior Olympics, this is also the time that athletes begin competing in the hammer throw.
Endurance	Running should be organic and playful. Energy system training (repeats, intensive tempo, heart rate work, and so forth) should be avoided. Races up to a mile are appropriate. Healthy 10-year-olds who are not necessarily distance runners should be able to continuously run 1/2 mile. Children in the distance races generally compete in events such as the 800-meter and mile run.	Children may begin running as much as three or four times a week at this stage. Be sure not to burn out children physically or mentally by making running into a chore. Try to teach athletes to enjoy running. Races are typically up to 2 miles.	In many places, early adolescents compete in races as long as 3 miles or 5,000 meters at this level. As running becomes more serious, work to create a balanced training program that includes flexibility and general strength work as well as some introductory energy system work (such as intervals, repeats, and fartlek training).

Track

You may be lucky enough to have the use of a new, all-weather track surface for your team practices—perhaps at a local college or high school. Or maybe your team uses an older cinder or dirt track. Regardless of the track surface, you can teach your athletes the fundamentals of the running events. Successful programs have been run without a track altogether. The important thing is that the athletes have a safe place to run, free of obstacles.

Track & Field Apparel

For practices, instruct your athletes to wear T-shirts and either shorts or running pants—basically, the same type of clothing they'd wear to a track meet, but not their official team uniform. Track and field apparel fits more snuggly than basketball or soccer gear. This helps the coach observe joint angles for technical instruction and allows for freedom of movement. Teach athletes to dress in layers when the weather is cool so they can remove sweatshirts and the like as they warm up throughout practice. For meets, many leagues and governing organizations require athletes to wear uniforms that are alike in color and style, especially for relay events. In most cases, this means your athletes should wear matching T-shirts or singlets. Athletes can wear shorts, pants, or tights, but they should all be the same color. Depending on your team and the competitions in your area, the rules regarding uniforms may be more or less strict.

During practices, athletes should usually wear good running shoes and should double-knot the laces to prevent them from coming untied, which can cause an athlete to trip. Specialty shoes such as spikes and those designed for specific field events are unnecessary for the youngest athletes and are not allowed in the Hershey program. Some parents may ask you about whether to buy these for their son or daughter. As athletes become more skilled, they will be ready for competition-style shoes. It may be difficult to find these locally, but most types of track and field shoes can be found in children's sizes from online retailers. Athletes with long hair should pull their hair back off their face with a headband or ponytail holder. In addition, don't allow athletes to wear jewelry or other metal objects.

The typical outdoor track has eight or nine running lanes that cover 400 meters in one lap. This means that the track is roughly four laps to one mile. Indoor tracks tend to be about half the size of outdoor tracks and are usually eight or more laps per mile. Generally speaking, these distances refer to the circumference while running in lane 1 of the track. The distance will be farther when running in a middle or outside lane. Because of this, the track should have several markings that indicate the "staggers" for starting various races. Figure 3.1 shows the markings for a typical track. Note that your track may be different. If the markings aren't clearly labeled on the track (e.g., "400-meter start"), ask an experienced coach or administrator if a chart or drawing exists that shows the markings.

Several aspects of the track shown in figure 3.1 are referred to using special track and field terminology. Here are a few definitions:

- *Common finish.* A straight white line near the end of one straightaway. Various races will use different starting lines but will finish at this standard point.

- *Acceleration zone.* This is a 10-meter area immediately before the exchange zone used for sprint relays. Outgoing runners may position themselves in this area so that they have more distance to build up speed before receiving the baton in the exchange zone. In the Hershey program, there is no acceleration zone; relay runners must be in their initial position in the exchange zone. Also called fly zone or international zone.

- *Exchange zone.* This area of the track designates where the baton may be legally passed during a relay race. It is marked by triangles spaced 20 meters apart.

- *Waterfall starting line.* The curved line used for the start of longer distance races. At the start, athletes may immediately break to the inside of the track as long as they do not impede other runners.

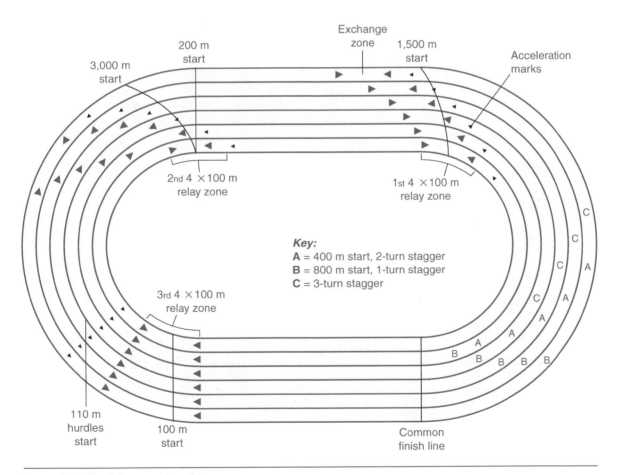

Figure 3.1   Track lanes and markings.

- *One-turn stagger.* These starting lines are used for shorter distance races or when a large number of runners are participating in a long-distance race. Runners stay in lanes or alleys for the first curve and break to the inside at the beginning of the first straightaway.
- *Two-turn stagger.* The 400-meter dash and some longer relays use starting lines measured out for both turns. For the dash, runners must stay in their lanes all the way around the track. For a two-turn stagger relay, runners break to the inside after the second turn.
- *Three-turn stagger.* These starting lines are used by older age groups in longer relays such as the mile or 1,600-meter relay. Breaking to the inside after the third turn allows the first exchange to happen in designated lanes for safety. By the second and third exchange, the runners are generally spread out so the baton pass can happen near the inside of the track.

Field Events

Each field event requires a special venue. In the Hershey's program, the field events include the standing long jump and the softball throw and are designed to require little specific equipment or facilities. This is especially helpful for school-based programs or for programs in areas where there aren't any track and field facilities. For example, the softball throw and the standing long jump can be practiced and contested nearly anywhere with open space. For USATF Junior Olympics, the field events all require a specific setup that may include landing mats, sand pits, a throwing ring, a runway, and marked sectors. Sample figures of each event can be found in chapters 9 and 10. Here are the most common field events for USATF Junior Olympics:

- Long jump and triple jump
- High jump
- Pole vault
- Shot put
- Discus
- Javelin

Long Jump and Triple Jump

The long jump and triple jump are contested in the horizontal jumping area. The area consists of a runway and a sand pit. The runway is generally 4 feet wide and between 100 and 150 feet long. A concrete or asphalt subsurface is covered with a synthetic material such as urethane to provide some cushioning and allow the spikes to grab. Take-off boards for the respective jumps are painted in white or constructed out of wood and implanted into the runway itself. In the case of a wooden take-off board, it is essential that the board is flush with the runway surface to prevent a tripping hazard. The sand itself is to be at least a foot deep and contained in a concrete or wooden framework. The surface of the sand is to be the same elevation as the runway.

High Jump

The competitive area for the high jump consists of an approach apron, a foam landing system, adustable standards, and a crossbar. The approach apron differs from the approach runways used in the other jumps. The apron is a wide open space that allows jumpers to approach from any angle. The surface is the same as the track. The landing system is made of sections of foam covered in vinyl and held together with buckles.

Pole Vault

The pole vault area includes a linear approach runway, a plant box, standards to hold the crossbar, and a foam landing system. The runway is very similar to the long jump, except instead of a sand pit at the end, there is a metal box built into the ground for the vaulter to plant the pole. The landing system includes sections that extend around the box and the standards for safety.

Shot Put

The shot put is contested in a venue that consists of a concrete circle and raised toeboard. The surface of the circle should have some traction, but is not to be overly rough. Often the 7-foot circle is simply painted on a square or rectangular concrete slab. In some cases the circle is described by a metal ring built into the concrete. The landing surface is usually a fine gravel as the implements do great damage to grass fields.

Discus

Typically, the discus is contested in a space that is shared with soccer or football fields. The implements cause little if any damage to the field so this can work if the coaches and athletes share a commitment to safety. There should never be discus practice or competition when any ball players are using the field. The area includes a concrete slab and circle similar to the shot put. The circle is 2.50 meters or 8 feet 2 inches. A "cage" surrounds the circle. The cage consists of poles and netting to prevent errant throws from landing outside the designated impact area. The designated impact area should be flagged off for competitions so that runners or spectators do not accidently enter the area.

Javelin

The javelin throw is contested from a runway. Generally the runway is made out of the same material as the track, although, in some cases the javelin is thrown off grass. The runway is between 100 and 150 feet and is described by white lines. At the end of the runway is a semi-circular foul line. The impact area is similar to the discus and the same safety precautions should be used.

Equipment and Implements

The standard pieces of equipment for track and field include hurdles, landing mats, starting blocks, batons, and throwing implements such as the shot put, discus, javelin, turbojavelin, and softball. How do you know when this equipment meets proper specifications and is in good repair? As a coach, you must examine the condition of each item you use. Also make sure that the pieces of equipment that athletes furnish themselves meet acceptable standards. Ensure that each athlete on your team is outfitted properly, and demonstrate to athletes how to properly use the equipment and implements. Following is additional information on the common equipment used in track and field:

Vertical Jump Landing Systems

For the vertical jumps—high jump and pole vault—you need to have legal landing systems, commonly called *pits*. Pits are large pieces of foam covered in vinyl and held together with buckles. The dimensions of the pits vary by developmental level. Older athletes should never attempt to jump into a pit that is designed for children. These landing systems are very expensive—vaulting pits can easily cost more than $15,000. Make sure to store and maintain them with care. Inspect the vinyl and buckles for damage and make sure the pieces are assembled correctly before each use.

Hurdles

Standard hurdles are L-shaped adjustable barriers that can be set to be from 30 to 42 inches high. The "L" shape allows them to easily tip over if an athlete makes contact while attempting to clear the barrier. Never allow athletes to go over hurdles set to be cleared from the other direction. This is extremely dangerous because the L shape will not allow the hurdle to tip over. For younger children, plastic hurdles that are 1 foot high can be purchased or made from PVC pipe; these low hurdles are a good way to expose children to the event.

Starting Blocks

Starting blocks consist of a center rail and adjustable pedals for an athlete to use as a pushing surface for the first movement in a short race. Smaller children can use smaller starting blocks because they are not able to generate significant amounts of force. As athletes develop and get bigger, they will need to use sturdy blocks that will not bend or break under the pressure of aggressive acceleration.

Throwing Implements

Shots, discs, javelins, and hammers are part of a well-rounded inventory. The specifics of each implement are discussed in chapter 10. It is a good idea to have some equipment that is reserved for competitions and specific practices. For general training, less expensive implements can be used.

Batons

Batons used in relays are plastic or aluminum tubes about one foot long. They must be smooth, with no dents or scratches that can assist in grip.

Poles

Pole vault poles are made from fiberglass and are available in a large range of sizes for athletes of all developmental levels. Sometimes, vaulting poles for advanced athletes mix carbon fibers with the fiberglass so that the pole is lighter and easier to carry down the runway. In addition, poles are classified by length and stiffness. Longer, stiffer poles are used by more experienced jumpers, whereas young athletes use smaller and softer poles. The stiffness rating is recorded on the pole in pounds and indicates the maximum athlete weight that the pole can support. For example, an athlete weighing 130 pounds must jump on a pole rated 130 or higher.

Tape Measures

Tape measures are important for practices as well as competitions. They are used not only to measure the distances of jumps and throws at track meets, but also to measure the approach run for the jumps and to measure sections of the track for running workouts. Short tape measures are okay for the jumps, but longer tapes are needed for the throws and to measure the intervals for sprint work.

Stopwatches

The stopwatch is an essential tool for the track coach. Some wristwatches and mobile phones have stopwatches, and these might suffice for some coaches. Many coaches find it more convenient to use a traditional stopwatch that is hung around the neck. When working with distance runners, coaches need a watch that can take several splits, especially if they are training a large group.

Starting Equipment

You will want to have some starting equipment for practicing starts with your athletes. This could be an actual starter's pistol or something more basic such as a "clapper" style starter or even a whistle.

Rakes and Brooms

Having rakes, shovels, and brooms at your facility may not seem as important as having some of the sport-specific equipment, but these items will help you to maintain safe jumping pits and clean throwing areas.

Cones

Plastic cones, similar to the orange ones used by your local street department, have a myriad of uses in youth track and field. You can use them to mark relay exchange zones more prominently, to set up drills in the infield, or to mark boundaries for warm-up games such as "tag."

Meet Entries

Some youth track and field programs place an emphasis on team scores at competitions, while others focus solely on individual performances. You will want to take this into consideration when planning meet entries. In some programs, the coach will make these decisions. Other coaches let parents sign their children up for their events. In this case, parents may ask for your advice. Either way, you should focus on creating a fun, balanced experience for each athlete at each competition.

As a coach, you should give each of your young athletes a chance to practice and compete in a variety of events. By trying different events, they'll have a better all-around experience and may stay more interested in the sport. Furthermore, they'll gain a better understanding of the many technical and tactical skills used in the sport. This will also help them appreciate the efforts of their teammates who compete in events they find difficult. Don't enter an athlete in too many similar events that could leave the athlete exhausted and possibly frustrated. If an athlete focuses on field events, you may want to sign that athlete up for one running event to provide balance, and vice versa.

Rules of Competition

Track and field rules are designed to make the events run smoothly and safely and to prevent individuals and teams from gaining an unfair advantage. Throw out the rules and a track and field meet can quickly turn chaotic. Following is an overview of some of the basic rules in track and field.

Running Etiquette and Rules

If you are new to coaching youth track and field, you may be surprised to learn that the youngest athletes often have a difficult time learning the most basic rule of the sprinting events: Stay in your lane! You should have your youngest athletes practice this until they have a good feel for "running etiquette." This includes knowing when they must stay in their own lane, when it is appropriate to "cut in," and how to safely and fairly pass another competitor. The general rule is that an athlete may not impede another runner. If an athlete cutting in front causes a competitor to break stride in order to avoid a collision, then the athlete has committed an infraction. To pass properly, a runner must be entirely ahead of other runners before cutting in front.

Starting Rules

Typically, three-command starts are used for dashes, and two-command starts are used for longer runs. The three commands are "on your marks," "set," and then the starting command (usually the report of a starter's pistol). At the "set" command, runners must immediately assume the position they will use for the start and remain very still. If any wiggling or shuffling occurs, the starter will tell the runners to stand; the starter will then warn the wiggler and go through the commands again. In the two-command start, the starter uses only the "take your marks" command and the starting signal.

Coaching Tip

Coaches should strongly encourage runners to focus on the finish line rather than on the other runners in the race. Turning the head to see where the competition is can cause a runner to slow down or even trip. All effort should be placed on moving directly forward toward the line.

For a fair start, all runners must hold still until the starting command. If a runner moves slightly before the sound of the gun, that runner is charged with a false start. The rules for false starts vary by organizing body; however, in the Hershey program, athletes are allowed one false start before disqualification.

Field Event Etiquette and Rules

The throwing events and the horizontal jumps share a similar competition format. Athletes are put into groups—referred to as *flights*—that consist of 6 to 12 athletes each. The competition rules of the organizers will determine how many attempts each athlete will have (usually three or four attempts). The athletes are called by the official when it is their turn to attempt their throw or jump. Athletes need to pay attention and be ready to compete when their name is called. Wasting time by removing warm-ups or engaging in practice moves can result in a foul. Fair attempts are measured and recorded, and fouls are recorded with an X.

Recording Field Event Attempts

A well-kept score sheet for the field events can tell you what happened on every attempt—the distance or height marked, how many attempts were required, and when fouls were committed. The host team will likely provide officials who will record the attempts to determine final standings. However, if you are a field event coach, you may prefer to keep track yourself so you can make notes during the meet. You could also ask an assistant coach or a parent to record the attempts if you prefer to focus on the competition.

Officials

Track and field officials are present at meets to enforce the rules of competition. At the youth level, meets might be run by parents and other volunteers. It takes a number of adults to run a safe and fair track meet. The number of officials will depend on the size and relative importance of the competition.

For events on the track, a clerk, starters, and timers are needed. The clerk checks the runners in and makes sure they line up for the right race and are positioned in the correct lane. The clerk usually has a "runner" who takes the starting list to the timers. At least one starter is required (sometimes two or three starters are needed). The starter calls the athletes to the line and issues commands to signal the beginning of the race. At the finish line, timers time each individual athlete and record the times and the finish order on the starting list.

For the field events, a minimum of two officials are needed to run each event. One person handles the clipboard, calls the athletes to compete, observes the attempt to determine if it is fair or foul, and measures and records the result. The second official holds the tape measure at the "zero" end and marks the place where either a throwing implement or a jumper lands. When more officials are available, the jobs of the first official can be broken up to make the event run more efficiently.

The scope and rules of the particular competition will determine the number of officials and specific assignments. For the USATF Junior Olympics program, competitions are usually run by the local association and they will provide officials. Hershey's program, because it is more of a grassroots organization, often relies on the help of parents and volunteers for their officiating needs and lists the following necessary officials:

Meet director	Finish timers (eight)
Meet referee	Head judge
Announcer	Head timer
Awards presenter	Starter
Recorder	Turn and land inspectors
Clerk of course	

Note that for the softball throw, a judge/measurer, recorder, and ball chaser are required. For the standing long jump, a judge/measurer and recorder are required.

4

Providing for Athletes' Safety

One of your young distance runners rounds the final curve, heading for the finish in first place. She crosses the line just before two other competitors. You stop cheering when you see your athlete collide with a spectator crossing the track. What do you do?

No coach wants to see athletes get hurt. But injury remains a reality of sport participation; consequently, you must be prepared to provide first aid when injuries occur and to protect yourself against unjustified lawsuits. Fortunately, coaches can institute many preventive measures to reduce the risk. In this chapter, we describe steps you can take to prevent injuries, first aid and emergency responses for when injuries occur, and your legal responsibilities as a coach.

Game Plan for Safety

You can't prevent all injuries from happening, but you can take preventive measures that give your athletes the best possible chance for injury-free participation. To help you create the safest possible environment for your athletes, we'll explore what you can do in these areas:

- Preseason physical examinations
- Physical conditioning
- Facilities and equipment inspection
- Inherent risks
- Proper supervision and record keeping
- Environmental conditions

Preseason Physical Examinations

We recommend that your athletes have a physical examination before participating in track and field. The exam should address the most likely areas of medical concern and identify youngsters at high risk. We also suggest that you ask athletes' parents or guardians to sign a participation agreement form (discussed in more detail later in this chapter) and an informed consent form to allow their children to be treated in case of an emergency. For a sample form, please see "Informed Consent Form" in appendix A on page 212.

Physical Conditioning

Athletes need to be in shape (or get in shape) to participate at the level expected. They must have adequate cardiorespiratory fitness and muscular fitness.

Cardiorespiratory fitness involves the body's ability to use oxygen and fuels efficiently to power muscle contractions. As athletes get in better shape, their bodies are able to more efficiently deliver oxygen to fuel muscles and carry off carbon dioxide and other wastes. At times, track and field will require lots of running and exertion. Youngsters who aren't as fit as their peers often overextend in trying to keep up, which can result in light-headedness, nausea, fatigue, and potential injury.

Try to remember that the athletes' goals are to participate, learn, and have fun. Therefore, you must keep the athletes active, attentive, and involved with every phase of practice. If you do, they will attain higher levels of cardiorespiratory fitness as the season progresses simply by taking part in practice. However, you should watch closely for signs of low cardiorespiratory fitness; don't let your athletes overdo it as they build their fitness. You might privately counsel youngsters who appear overly winded, suggesting that they train outside of practice (under proper supervision) to increase their fitness.

Muscular fitness encompasses strength, muscular endurance, power, speed, and flexibility. This type of fitness is affected by physical maturity as well as strength training and other types of training. Your athletes will likely exhibit a relatively wide range of muscular fitness. Those who have greater muscular fitness will be able to run faster and throw farther. They will also sustain fewer muscular injuries, and any injuries that do occur will tend to be minor. And in case of injury, recovery is faster in athletes with higher levels of muscular fitness.

Two other components of fitness and injury prevention are the warm-up and the cool-down. Although young bodies are generally very limber, they can become tight through inactivity. The warm-up should address each muscle group and should elevate the heart rate in preparation for strenuous activity. Athletes should warm up for 5 to 10 minutes using a combination of light running, skipping, easy jumping, and loosening moves. As practice winds down, slow athletes' heart rates with an easy jog or walk. Then have the athletes stretch for 5 minutes to help prevent tight muscles before the next practice or competition.

> **Coaching Tip**
> Younger athletes may not be aware of when they need a break for water and a short rest; therefore, you need to work breaks into your practice schedules. In addition, you should have water available at all times during the practice session. The athletes will have different hydration needs, and this will allow them to grab a drink when they need it, with the added benefit of reducing the need for long water breaks during the practice session.

Facilities and Equipment Inspection

Another way to prevent injuries is to regularly examine the surfaces on which your athletes practice. Remove hazards, report conditions you cannot remedy, and request maintenance as necessary. If unsafe conditions exist, you should either make adaptations to prevent risk to your athletes' safety or stop the practice or competition until safe conditions have been restored. You can also prevent injuries by checking the quality and fit of uniforms, practice attire, and any protective equipment used by your athletes. Refer to the "Facilities and Equipment Checklist" in appendix A (page 210) to guide you in verifying that facilities and equipment are safe.

Inherent Risks

As a coach, you must warn athletes of the inherent risks involved in participating in track and field, because "failure to warn" is one of the most successful arguments in lawsuits against coaches. So, thoroughly explain the inherent risks of track and field, and make sure each athlete knows, understands, and appreciates those risks. You can learn more about inherent risks by talking with your league administrators.

The preseason parent orientation meeting is a good opportunity to explain the risks of the sport to both parents and athletes. It is also a good time to have both the athletes and their parents sign a participation agreement form or waiver releasing you from liability should an injury occur. You should work with your park district or league when creating these forms or waivers, and legal counsel should review them before presentation. These forms or waivers do not relieve you of responsibility for your athletes' well-being, but they are recommended by lawyers and may help you in the event of a lawsuit.

Proper Supervision and Record Keeping

To ensure athletes' safety, you must provide both general and specific supervision. *General supervision* means you are in the area of activity so you can see and hear what is happening. You should be

- at the track and field facility and in position to supervise the athletes even before the formal practice begins,
- immediately accessible to the activity and able to oversee the entire activity,
- alert to conditions that may be dangerous to athletes and ready to take action to protect athletes,
- able to react immediately and appropriately to emergencies, and
- present at the track and field facility until the last athlete has been picked up after the practice or competition.

Specific supervision is the direct supervision of an activity during practice. For example, you should provide specific supervision when you teach new skills and should continue it until your athletes understand the requirements of the activity, the risks involved, and their own ability to perform in light of these risks. You must also provide specific supervision when you notice athletes breaking rules or notice a change in the condition of your athletes. As a general rule, the more dangerous the activity, the more specific the supervision required. This suggests that more specific supervision is required with younger and less experienced athletes, and also for older athletes who are learning and practicing more dangerous skills, such as hurdling and the vertical jumps.

As part of your supervision duty, you are expected to foresee potentially dangerous situations and to be positioned to help prevent them. This requires that you know track and field well, especially the rules that are intended to provide for safety. Prohibit dangerous horseplay, and hold training sessions only under safe weather conditions. These specific supervisory activities, performed consistently, will make the environment safer for your athletes and will help protect you from liability if a mishap occurs.

For further protection, keep records of your season plans, practice plans, and athletes' injuries. Season and practice plans come in handy when you need evidence that athletes have been taught certain skills, whereas accurate, detailed injury report forms offer protection against unfounded lawsuits. Ask for these forms from your sponsoring organization (see page 213 in appendix A for a sample injury report form), and hold onto these records for several years so that an old injury doesn't come back to haunt you.

> **Coaching Tip**
> Common sense tells us that it's easier to provide specific supervision to a smaller group of athletes, regardless of age. Enlist the help of assistant coaches so that you can divide your team into smaller groups. This will help ensure that athletes can practice skills in a safe environment. The more adults who can help supervise, the better the athletes can learn and perform the necessary skills. In addition, smaller groups allow each coach to provide more direct feedback to athletes.

Environmental Conditions

Most health problems caused by environmental factors are related to excessive heat or cold, although you should also consider other environmental factors such as severe weather and air pollution. A little thought about the potential problems and a little effort to ensure adequate protection for your athletes will prevent most serious emergencies related to environmental conditions.

Heat

On hot, humid days the body has difficulty cooling itself. Because the air is already saturated with water vapor (humidity), sweat doesn't evaporate as easily. Therefore, body sweat is a less effective cooling agent, and the body retains extra heat. Hot, humid environments put athletes at risk of heat exhaustion and heatstroke (see more on these in "Serious Injuries" on pages 45-47). And if *you* think it's hot or humid, it's worse for the kids, not only because they're more active but also because kids under the age of 12 have more difficulty regulating their body temperature than adults do. To provide

Coaching Tip

Encourage athletes to drink plenty of water before, during, and after practice. Water makes up 45 to 65 percent of a youngster's body weight, and even a small amount of water loss can cause severe consequences in the body's systems. It doesn't have to be hot and humid for athletes to become dehydrated, nor is thirst an accurate indicator. In fact, by the time athletes are aware of their thirst, they are long overdue for a drink.

for athletes' safety in hot or humid conditions, take the following preventive measures:

- Monitor weather conditions and adjust practices accordingly. Table 4.1 shows the specific air temperatures and humidity percentages that can be hazardous.

- Acclimatize athletes to exercising in high heat and humidity. Athletes can adjust to high heat and humidity in 7 to 10 days. During this period, hold practices at low to moderate activity levels, and give the athletes fluid breaks every 20 minutes.

- Switch to light clothing. Athletes should wear shorts and white T-shirts.

- Identify and monitor athletes who are prone to heat illness. This would include athletes who are overweight, heavily muscled, or out of shape and athletes who work excessively hard or have suffered previous heat illness. Closely monitor these athletes, and give them fluid breaks every 15 to 20 minutes.

- Make sure athletes replace fluids lost through sweat. Encourage athletes to drink 17 to 20 ounces of fluid 2 to 3 hours before practices or competitions and 7 to 10 ounces every 20 minutes during practice and after practice. Afterward they should drink 16 to 24 ounces of fluid for every pound lost during exercise. Fluids such as water and sports drinks are preferable during competitions and practices (suggested intakes are based on NATA [National Athletic Trainers' Association] recommendations).

- Encourage athletes to replenish electrolytes, such as sodium (salt) and potassium, that are lost through sweat. The best way to replace these nutrients—as well as others such as carbohydrate (for energy) and protein (for muscle building)—is by eating a balanced diet.

Table 4.1   Warm-Weather Precautions

Temperature (°F)	Humidity	Precautions
80-90	<70%	Monitor athletes prone to heat illness
80-90	>70%	5-minute rest after 30 minutes of practice
90-100	<70%	5-minute rest after 30 minutes of practice
90-100	>70%	Short practices in evenings or early morning

Cold

When a person is exposed to cold weather, body temperature starts to drop below normal. To counteract this reaction, the body shivers to create heat and reduces blood flow to the extremities to conserve heat in the core of the body. But no matter how effective its natural heating mechanism is, the body will better withstand cold temperatures if it is prepared to handle them. To reduce the risk of cold-related illnesses, keep athletes active to maintain body heat, and make sure they wear appropriate protective clothing. Also monitor the windchill factor because it can drastically affect the severity of athletes' responses to the weather. The windchill factor index is shown in figure 4.1.

Severe Weather

Severe weather refers to a host of potential dangers, including lightning storms, tornadoes, hail, and heavy rains. Lightning is of special concern because it can come up quickly and can cause great harm or even kill. For each 5-second count from the flash of lightning to the bang of thunder, lightning is one mile away. A count of 10 seconds means lightning is two miles away; a count of 15 seconds indicates lightning is three miles away. A practice or competition should be stopped for the day if lightning is six miles away or closer (30 seconds or fewer from flash to bang). In addition to these suggestions, your school, league, or state association may have additional rules that you will want to consider in severe weather.

Safe places to take cover when lightning strikes include fully enclosed metal vehicles with the windows up, enclosed buildings, and low ground (under cover of bushes, if possible). It's not safe to be near metal objects such as flagpoles, fences, light poles, and metal bleachers. Also avoid trees, water, and open fields.

	Temperature (°F)								
	0	5	10	15	20	25	30	35	40
	Flesh may freeze within one minute								
40	-55	-45	-35	-30	-20	-15	-5	0	10
35	-50	-40	-35	-30	-20	-10	-5	5	10
30	-50	-40	-30	-25	-20	-10	0	5	10
25	-45	-35	-30	-20	-15	-5	0	10	15
20	-35	-30	-25	-15	-10	0	5	10	20
15	-30	-25	-20	-10	-5	0	10	15	25
10	-20	-15	-10	0	5	10	15	20	30
5	-5	0	5	10	15	20	25	30	35

Wind speed (mph)

Windchill temperature (°F)

Figure 4.1   Windchill factor index.

Cancel practice when under a tornado watch or warning. If you are practicing or competing when a tornado is nearby, you should get inside a building if possible. If you cannot get into a building, lie in a ditch or other low-lying area, or crouch near a strong building. Use your arms to protect your head and neck, and instruct athletes to do the same.

The keys to handling severe weather are caution and prudence. Don't try to get that last 10 minutes of practice in if lightning is on the horizon. Don't continue to practice in heavy rain. Many storms can strike both quickly and ferociously. Respect the weather and play it safe.

Air Pollution

Poor air quality and smog can present real dangers to your athletes. Both short- and long-term lung damage are possible from participating in unsafe air. Although it's true that participating in clean air is not possible in many areas, restricting activity is recommended when the air quality ratings are lower than moderate or when there is a smog alert. Your local health department or air quality control board can inform you of the air quality ratings for your area and when restricting activities is recommended.

Responding to Athletes' Injuries

No matter how good and thorough your prevention program is, injuries most likely will occur. When injury does strike, chances are you will be the one in charge. The severity and nature of the injury will determine how actively involved you'll be in treating it. But regardless of how seriously an athlete is hurt, it is your responsibility to know what steps to take. Therefore, you must be prepared to take appropriate action and provide basic emergency care when an injury occurs.

Being Prepared

Being prepared to provide basic emergency care involves many things, including being trained in cardiopulmonary resuscitation (CPR) and first aid and having an emergency action plan.

CPR and First Aid Training

We recommend that all coaches receive CPR and first aid training from a nationally recognized organization such as the National Safety Council, the American Heart Association, the American Red Cross, or the American Sport Education Program (ASEP). You should be certified based on a practical test and a written test of knowledge. CPR training should include pediatric and adult basic life support and obstructed airway procedures.

First Aid Kit

A well-stocked first aid kit should include the following:

- Antibacterial soap or wipes
- Arm sling
- Athletic tape—one and a half inches wide
- Bandage scissors
- Bandage strips—assorted sizes
- Blood spill kit
- Cell phone
- Contact lens case
- Cotton swabs
- Elastic wraps—3 inches, 4 inches, and 6 inches
- Emergency blanket
- Examination gloves—latex free
- Eye patch
- Foam rubber—one-eighth inch, one-fourth inch, and one-half inch
- Insect sting kit
- List of emergency phone numbers
- Mirror
- Moleskin
- Nail clippers
- Oral thermometer (to determine if an athlete has a fever caused by illness)
- Penlight
- Petroleum jelly
- Plastic bags for crushed ice
- Prewrap (underwrap for tape)
- Rescue breathing or CPR face mask
- Safety glasses (for first aiders)
- Safety pins
- Saline solution for eyes
- Sterile gauze pads—3-inch and 4-inch squares (preferably nonstick)
- Sterile gauze rolls
- Sunscreen—sun protection factor (SPF) 30 or greater
- Tape adherent and tape remover
- Tongue depressors
- Tooth saver kit
- Triangular bandages
- Tweezers

Adapted, by permission, from M. Flegel, 2004, *Sport first aid*, 3rd ed. (Champaign, IL: Human Kinetics), 20.

Emergency Plan

An emergency plan is the final step in being prepared to take appropriate action for serious injuries. The plan calls for three steps:

1. *Evaluate the injured athlete.*

   Use your CPR and first aid training to guide you. Be sure to keep these certifications up-to-date. Practice your skills frequently to keep them fresh and ready to use if and when you need them.

2. *Call the appropriate medical personnel.*

   If possible, delegate the responsibility of seeking medical help to another calm and responsible adult who attends all practices and competitions. Write out a list of emergency phone numbers, and keep it with you at practices and competitions. Include the following phone numbers:

   - Rescue unit
   - Hospital
   - Physician
   - Police
   - Fire department

   Take each athlete's emergency information to every practice and competition (see "Emergency Information Card" in appendix A on page 214). This information includes the person to contact in case of an emergency, what types of medications the athlete is using, what types of drugs the athlete is allergic to, and so on.

   Give an emergency response card (see "Emergency Response Card" in appendix A on page 215) to the contact person calling for emergency assistance. Having this information ready should help the contact person remain calm. You must also complete an injury report form (see "Injury Report Form" in appendix A on page 213) and keep it on file for every injury that occurs.

3. *Provide first aid.*

   If medical personnel are not on hand at the time of the injury, you should provide first aid care to the extent of your qualifications. Again, although your CPR and first aid training will guide you, you must remember the following:

   - Do not move the injured athlete if the injury is to the head, neck, or back; if a large joint (ankle, knee, elbow, shoulder) is dislocated; or if the pelvis, a rib, or an arm or leg is fractured.
   - Calm the injured athlete, and keep others away from him as much as possible.
   - Evaluate whether the athlete's breathing has stopped or is irregular, and if necessary, clear the airway with your fingers.

- Administer CPR as directed in the CPR certification course recommended by your school, league, or state association.
- Remain with the athlete until medical personnel arrive.

Emergency Steps

You must have a clear, well-rehearsed emergency action plan. You want to be sure you are prepared in case of an emergency because every second counts. Your emergency plan should follow this sequence:

1. Check the athlete's level of consciousness.
2. Send a contact person to call the appropriate medical personnel and to locate or call the athlete's parents.
3. Send someone to wait for the rescue team and direct them to the injured athlete.
4. Assess the injury.
5. Administer first aid.
6. Assist emergency medical personnel in preparing the athlete for transportation to a medical facility.
7. Appoint someone to go with the athlete if the parents are not available. This person should be responsible, calm, and familiar with the athlete. Assistant coaches or other parents are best for this job.
8. Complete an injury report form while the incident is fresh in your mind (see page 213 in appendix A).

Taking Appropriate Action

Proper CPR and first aid training, a well-stocked first aid kit, and an emergency plan help prepare you to take appropriate action when an injury occurs. In the previous section, we mentioned the importance of providing first aid to the extent of your qualifications. Don't "play doctor" with injuries; sort out minor injuries that you can treat from those that need medical attention. Now let's look at the appropriate action for minor injuries and more serious injuries.

Minor Injuries

Although no injury seems minor to the person experiencing it, most injuries are neither life threatening nor severe enough to restrict participation. When these injuries occur, you can take an active role in their initial treatment.

Scrapes and Cuts   When one of your athletes has an open wound, the first thing you should do is put on a pair of disposable latex-free examination gloves or some other effective blood barrier. Then follow these four steps:

1. Stop the bleeding by applying direct pressure with a clean dressing to the wound and elevating it. The athlete may be able to apply this pressure while you put on your gloves. Do not remove the dressing if it becomes soaked with blood. Instead, place an additional dressing on top of the one already in place. If bleeding continues, elevate the injured area above the heart and maintain pressure.

2. Cleanse the wound thoroughly once the bleeding is controlled. A good rinsing with a forceful stream of water, and perhaps light scrubbing with soap, will help prevent infection.

3. Protect the wound with sterile gauze or a bandage strip. If the athlete continues to participate, apply protective padding over the injured area.

4. Remove and dispose of gloves carefully to keep yourself (or anyone else) from coming into contact with blood.

For bloody noses not associated with serious facial injury, have the athlete sit and lean slightly forward. Then pinch the athlete's nostrils shut. If the bleeding continues for several minutes, or if the athlete has a history of nosebleeds, seek medical assistance.

Strains and Sprains   The physical demands of participating in track and field often result in injury to the muscles or tendons (strains) or to the ligaments (sprains). When your athletes suffer minor strains or sprains, you should immediately apply the PRICE method of injury care:

P   Protect the athlete and the injured body part from further danger or trauma.

R   Rest the injured area to avoid further damage and to foster healing.

I   Ice the area to reduce swelling and pain.

C   Compress the area by securing an ice bag in place with an elastic wrap.

E   Elevate the injury above heart level to keep the blood from pooling in the area.

Bumps and Bruises   Inevitably, athletes make contact with each other or with the ground. If the force applied to a body part at impact is great enough, a bump or bruise will result. Many athletes continue to participate with such sore spots, but if the bump or bruise is large and painful, you should take appropriate action. Again, use the PRICE method for injury care, and monitor the injury. If swelling, discoloration, and pain have lessened, the athlete may resume participation with protective padding; if not, the athlete should be examined by a physician.

Serious Injuries

Head, neck, and back injuries; fractures; and injuries that cause an athlete to lose consciousness are among a class of injuries that you cannot and should not try to treat yourself. In these cases, you should follow the emergency plan outlined on page 42. We do want to examine more closely, however, your role in preventing and attending to heat cramps, heat exhaustion, and heatstroke. Additionally, please refer to figure 4.2 for an illustrative example of the signs and symptoms associated with heat exhaustion and heatstroke.

Coaching Tip

You shouldn't let a fear of acquired immune deficiency syndrome (AIDS) and other communicable diseases stop you from helping an athlete. You are at risk only if you allow contaminated blood to come in contact with an open wound on your body, so the examination gloves that you wear will protect you from AIDS if one of your athletes carries this disease. Check with your sport director, your league, or the Centers for Disease Control and Prevention (CDC) for more information about protecting yourself and your participants from AIDS.

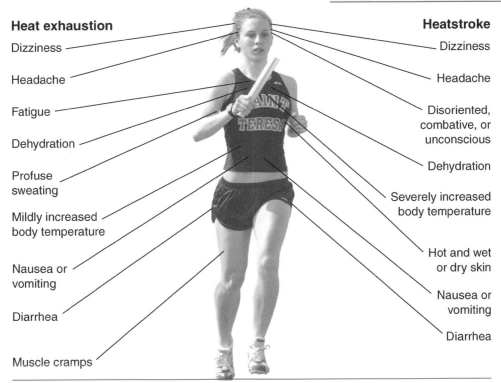

Heat exhaustion

Dizziness

Headache

Fatigue

Dehydration

Profuse sweating

Mildly increased body temperature

Nausea or vomiting

Diarrhea

Muscle cramps

Heatstroke

Dizziness

Headache

Disoriented, combative, or unconscious

Dehydration

Severely increased body temperature

Hot and wet or dry skin

Nausea or vomiting

Diarrhea

Figure 4.2   Signs and symptoms of heat exhaustion and heatstroke.

Heat Cramps   Tough practices combined with heat stress and substantial fluid loss from sweating can provoke muscle cramps commonly known as *heat cramps*. Cramping is most common when the weather is hot. Depending on your location, it may be hot early in the season, which can be problematic because athletes may be less conditioned and less adapted to heat. In other locations, it may be hot later in the season, when athletes are better conditioned but still not used to participating in high temperatures. A cramp, a severe tightening of the muscle, can drop athletes and prevent continued participation. Dehydration, electrolyte loss, and fatigue are the contributing factors. The immediate treatment is to have the athlete cool off, replace fluids lost through activity, and slowly stretch the contracted muscle. The athlete may resume participation later that same day or the next day provided the cramp doesn't cause a muscle strain.

Heat Exhaustion   Heat exhaustion is a shocklike condition caused by strenuous activity combined with heat stress. This, in addition to dehydration and electrolyte depletion, does not allow the body to keep up. Symptoms include fatigue, dizziness, headache, nausea, vomiting, diarrhea, and muscle cramps. Difficulty continuing activity, profuse sweating, and mildly increased body temperature are key signs of heat exhaustion.

An athlete suffering from heat exhaustion should rest in a cool (shaded or air-conditioned) area with her legs propped above heart level; remove excess clothing and equipment; drink cool fluids, particularly those containing electrolytes (if not nauseated); and apply ice to the neck, back, or abdomen to help cool the body. If you believe that an athlete is suffering from heat exhaustion, seek medical attention. Under no conditions should the athlete return to activity that day. In this situation, we recommend that the athlete not return to activity until she has a written release from a physician.

Heatstroke   Heatstroke is a life-threatening condition in which the body stops sweating and body temperature rises dangerously high. It results from the continuation of strenuous activity in extreme temperatures. Heatstroke occurs when dehydration and electrolyte depletion cause a malfunction in the body's temperature control center in the brain. Symptoms include fatigue, dizziness, confusion, irritability, hysteria, nausea, vomiting, diarrhea, and the feeling of being extremely hot. Signs include hot and wet or dry skin; rapid pulse and rapid breathing; and possible seizures, unconsciousness, or respiratory or cardiac arrest.

If you suspect that an athlete is suffering from heatstroke, send for emergency medical assistance immediately, and cool the athlete as quickly as possible. Remove excess clothing and equipment, and cool the athlete's body with cool, wet towels; by pouring cool water over the athlete; or by placing the athlete in a cold bath. Apply ice packs to the armpits, neck, back, abdomen, and between the legs. If the athlete is conscious, give him cool fluids to drink. If the athlete is unconscious or falls unconscious, place the athlete on his side to allow fluids and vomit to drain from the mouth. An athlete who has suffered heatstroke may not return to the team until he has a written release from a physician.

Protecting Yourself

When one of your athletes is injured, naturally your first concern is the athlete's well-being. Your desire to help youngsters, after all, was what made you decide to coach. Unfortunately, you must also consider something else: Can you be held liable for the injury?

From a legal standpoint, a coach must fulfill nine duties. We've discussed all but planning in this chapter (planning is discussed in chapters 5 and 13). The following is a summary of your legal duties:

1. Provide a safe environment.
2. Properly plan the activity.
3. Provide adequate and proper equipment.
4. Match athletes appropriately.
5. Warn of inherent risks in the sport.
6. Supervise the activity closely.
7. Evaluate athletes for injury or incapacitation.
8. Know emergency procedures, CPR, and first aid.
9. Keep adequate records.

In addition to fulfilling these nine legal duties, you should check your organization's insurance coverage and your own personal insurance coverage to make sure these policies will properly protect you from liability.

5

Making Practices
Fun and Practical

n the past, we have placed too much emphasis on learning skills and not enough on learning how to perform skillfully—that is, how to use those skills in competition. The games approach (which is based on Alan Launder's book *Play Practice*), in contrast to the traditional approach, emphasizes learning what to do first, then how to do it. Moreover, the games approach lets kids discover what to do, not by your telling them but by their experiencing it. It is a guided discovery method of teaching that empowers your kids to solve the problems that arise, which is a large part of the fun in learning.

On the surface, it would seem to make sense to introduce track and field using the traditional approach—by first teaching the basic skills of an event and then how to use those skills in competition. But this approach has been shown to have disadvantages. First, it teaches the skills of the sport out of the context of competition. Kids may learn to grip the discus and assume some of the positions, but they often find it difficult to use these skills when the official calls their name and they have to try to throw for distance in competition. Second, learning skills by doing drills outside of the context of the competition is downright boring. The single biggest turnoff in sports is overorganized instruction that deprives kids of their intrinsic desire to compete.

The games approach adapted for track and field could be described as a four-step process:

1. Stage a modified activity.
2. Help athletes understand the activity.
3. Teach the skills of the activity.
4. Practice the skills in another modified activity.

Step 1: Stage a Modified Activity

It's the first day of practice; some of the kids are eager to get started, while others are obviously apprehensive. Some have never been to a track meet, most don't know the rules, and few know anything about the techniques used in the field events. What do you do?

If you used the traditional approach, you would start with a quick warm-up activity, then perhaps begin teaching the parts of one of the field events, such as the discus throw (grip, release, body position and movements, and so forth). With the games approach, however, you begin by allowing athletes to participate in a modified activity that is developmentally appropriate for the level of the athletes and also designed to focus on learning a specific part of a track and field event.

Modifying the activity lets you emphasize a limited number of technical aspects. This is one way to "guide" your players to discover certain methods that will improve performance. For instance, when teaching the discus, you could incorporate a simple game that challenges athletes to bowl the discus at a cone set as a target 5 to 10 meters away. The goal of the activity is to roll the implement along the ground so that it lands close to the cone. Executing the activity this way forces children to think about what they need to do to make the discus spin off the finger and go toward an intended target.

Activities Checklist

When developing activities for your youth track and field program, here are a few questions that you should ask yourself:

- Are the activities fun?
- Are the activities organized?
- Are the athletes involved in the activities?
- Do the activities require the athletes to use creativity and decision making?
- Are the spaces used appropriate for the activities?
- Is your feedback appropriate?
- Are there implications for a track and field event?

Step 2: Help Athletes Understand the Activity

As your players are participating in a modified competition, you should look for the right spot to "freeze" the action, step in, and ask questions about errors that you're seeing. When you do this, you help the athletes better understand the objective of the event, what they must do to achieve that objective, and also what skills they must use.

Asking the right questions is a very important part of your teaching. Essentially, you'll be asking your athletes—often literally—"What do you need to do to succeed in this situation?" Sometimes athletes simply need to gain more experience, or you may need to modify the task further so that it is even easier for them to discover what they need to do. It may take more patience on your part, but it's a powerful way for athletes to learn. For example, assume your athletes are participating in an activity in which the objective is to clear a high jump crossbar (set at a low height) 10 times in a row without knocking the bar down. Interrupt the action and ask the following questions:

- What are you supposed to do in this activity?
- What do you have to do to keep jumping consistently?
- What happens to your emotions as you get close to 10 in a row?
- How do you respond after failed attempts?

Coaching Tip

If your athletes have trouble understanding what to do, you can phrase your questions to let the athletes choose between two options. For example, if you ask, "What's the best way to correct your approach when you hit the bar on the way up immediately after takeoff?" and get an answer such as "Move my starting mark," then ask, "Do you move it forward or back?"

At first, asking the right questions might seem difficult because your athletes have little or no experience with the sport. And, if you've learned sport through the traditional approach, you'll be tempted to tell your athletes how to execute the skill rather than waste time asking questions. When using the games approach, however, you must resist this powerful temptation to tell your athletes what to do.

Instead, through modified activities and skillful questioning on your part, your athletes should come to realize on their own that tactical awareness and appropriate fundamentals, intensity, and emotional control are essential for success. Just as important, instead of telling them what the critical skills are, you led them to this discovery, which is a crucial part of the games approach.

Step 3: Teach the Skills of the Activity

Only when your athletes recognize the skills they need to be successful do you want to teach these skills through activities focused on specific track and field situations. This is when you use a more traditional approach to teaching sport skills, the IDEA approach, which we will describe in chapter 6. This type of teaching breaks down the skills of the events. It should be implemented early in the season so that athletes can begin attaining skills, which will make track more fun.

Step 4: Practice the Skills in Another Activity

As a coach, you want your athletes to experience success as they're learning skills, and the best way for them to experience this success early on is for you to create an advantage for the athletes. Once the athletes have practiced the skill, as outlined in step 3, you can then have them participate in another activity—this time slightly more challenging but with an advantage (e.g., instead of having the athletes clear 10 crossbars in a row, raise the bar slightly and have them clear it 5 consecutive times). This setup (requiring fewer successful jumps in a row) will make it more likely that your athletes will be able to successfully reach the goal.

Some track and field skills don't easily lend themselves to modified activities. For example, sometimes the basic mechanics of turning with the discus, planting a pole vault, or clearing the hurdles are best taught with individual attention to each athlete, often as athletes practice with a partner. However, throwing for distance, jumping for height or distance, and running for speed are ideal for modified competition.

As athletes develop and improve their skills, however, you may not need to provide an advantage. For example, clearing a crossbar set at a low height will eventually become too easy and won't challenge your athletes to hone their skills. When this time comes, you can lessen the advantage, or you may even decide that the athletes are ready to practice the skill in regular competition. The key is to set up situations where your athletes experience success yet are challenged in doing so. This will take careful monitoring on your part, but having kids compete in modified activities as they are learning skills is a very effective way of helping them learn and improve.

And that's the games approach. Your athletes will get to be more involved and engaged in practice, and once they learn how the skills fit into their performance and enjoyment of the competition, they'll be more motivated to work on those skills—which will help them to be successful.

Teaching and Shaping Skills

Coaching track and field is about teaching skills, fitness, and values to kids. It's also about coaching athletes before, during, and after competitions. Teaching and coaching are closely related, but there are important differences. In this chapter, we focus on principles of teaching, especially on teaching technical and tactical skills. But these principles apply to teaching values and fitness concepts as well. Armed with these principles, you will be able to design effective and efficient practices and will understand how to deal with misbehavior. Then you will be able to teach the skills that are necessary to be successful in track and field (these skills are outlined in chapters 7 through 11).

Teaching Track and Field Skills

Many people believe that the only qualification needed to teach a skill is to have performed it. Although it's helpful to have performed the skill, teaching it successfully requires much more than that. And even if you haven't performed the skill before, you can still learn to teach successfully with the useful acronym IDEA:

I   Introduce the skill.

D   Demonstrate the skill.

E   Explain the skill.

A   Attend to athletes practicing the skill.

Introduce the Skill

Athletes, especially those who are young and inexperienced, need to know what skill they are learning and why they are learning it. You should therefore use the following three steps every time you introduce a skill to your athletes:

1. Get your athletes' attention.
2. Name the skill.
3. Explain the importance of the skill.

Get Your Athletes' Attention

Because youngsters are easily distracted, you should do something to get their attention. Some coaches use interesting news items or stories. Others use jokes. And still others simply project enthusiasm to get their athletes to listen. Whatever method you use, speak slightly above your normal volume, and look your athletes in the eye when you speak.

Also, position athletes so they can see and hear you. Arrange the athletes in two or three evenly spaced rows, facing you. (Make sure they aren't looking into the sun or at a distracting activity.) Then ask whether all of them can see you before you begin to speak.

Name the Skill

More than one common name may exist for the skill you are introducing, but you should decide as a staff before the start of the season which one you'll use (and then stick with it). This will help prevent confusion and enhance communication among your athletes. When you introduce the new skill, call it by name several times so that the athletes automatically correlate the name with the skill in later discussions.

Explain the Importance of the Skill

As Rainer Martens, the founder of the American Sport Education Program (ASEP), has said, "The most difficult aspect of coaching is this: Coaches must learn to let athletes learn. Sport skills should be taught so they have meaning to the child, not just meaning to the coach." Although the importance of a skill may be apparent to you, your athletes may be less able to see how the skill will help them become better athletes. Give them a reason for learning the skill, and describe how the skill relates to more advanced techniques.

Demonstrate the Skill

The demonstration step is the most important part of teaching a sport skill to athletes who may never have done anything closely resembling the skill. They need a picture, not just words, so they can see how the skill is performed. If you are unable to perform the skill correctly, ask an assistant coach, one of your athletes, or someone more skilled to perform the demonstration.

These tips will help make your demonstrations more effective:

- Use correct form.
- Demonstrate the skill several times.
- Slow the action, if possible, during one or two performances so athletes can see every movement involved in the skill.
- Perform the skill at different angles so your athletes can get a full perspective of it.
- Demonstrate the skill with both sides of the body.

Explain the Skill

Athletes learn more effectively when they're given a brief explanation of the skill along with the

Coaching Tip

You may want to write out in detail each skill you will teach. This can help clarify what you will say and how you will demonstrate and teach each skill to your athletes.

demonstration. You should use simple terms, and if possible, relate the skill to previously learned skills. Ask your athletes whether they understand your description. A good technique is to ask the team to repeat your explanation. Ask questions such as, "What are you going to do first?" and "Then what?" If athletes look confused or uncertain, you should repeat your explanation and demonstration. If possible, use different words so your athletes get a chance to try to understand the skill from a different perspective.

Complex skills are often better understood when they are explained in more manageable parts. For instance, if you want to teach your athletes how to high jump, you might take the following steps:

1. Show them a correct performance of the entire skill.

2. Break down the skill and point out its component parts to your athletes.

3. Have athletes perform each of the component skills you have already taught them, such as running the curve and the penultimate step.

4. After athletes have demonstrated their ability to perform the separate parts of the skill in sequence, reexplain the entire skill.

5. Have athletes practice the skill in meetlike conditions.

Coaching Tip

Technology improvements have created an opportunity to bring new demonstration methods to the track or field. A variety of track and field DVDs are on the market, so consider using them as a tool to show athletes how to perform skills. This method can be especially useful if you have difficulty demonstrating a particular skill or locating someone who can demonstrate it for you. DVDs are very effective with older athletes, who are better able to transfer the skills they see on the screen to their own performance.

Young athletes have short attention spans, and a long demonstration or explanation of a skill may cause them to lose focus. Therefore, you should spend no more than a few minutes altogether on the introduction, demonstration, and explanation phases. Then involve the athletes in activities that call on them to perform the skill.

Attend to Athletes Practicing the Skill

If the skill you selected was within your athletes' capabilities and you have done an effective job of introducing, demonstrating, and explaining it, your athletes should be ready to attempt the skill. Some athletes, especially those in younger age groups, may need to be physically guided through the movements during their first few attempts. Walking unsure athletes through the skill in this way will help them gain confidence to perform the skill on their own.

Your teaching duties, though, don't end when all your athletes have demonstrated that they understand how to perform a skill. In fact, your teaching role is just beginning as you help your athletes improve their skills.

How to Properly Run Your Activities

Before performing activities that teach technique, you should do the following:

- Name the activity.
- Explain the skill or skills to be taught.
- Position the athletes correctly.
- Explain what the activity will accomplish.
- Identify the command that will start the activity.
- Identify the command that will end the activity, such as a whistle.

Once the activity has been introduced and repeated a few times in this manner, you will find that merely calling out the name of the activity is sufficient; your athletes will automatically line up in the proper position to practice the skill.

A significant part of your teaching consists of closely observing the hit-and-miss trial performances of your athletes. You will shape athletes' skills by detecting errors and correcting them using positive feedback. Keep in mind that your positive feedback will have a great influence on your athletes' motivation to practice and improve their performances.

Remember, too, that some athletes may need individual instruction. So set aside a time before, during, or after practice to give individual help.

Helping Athletes Improve Skills

After you have successfully taught your athletes the fundamentals of a skill, your focus will be on helping them improve the skill. Athletes learn skills and improve on them at different rates, so don't get frustrated if progress seems slow. Instead, help them improve by shaping their skills and detecting and correcting errors.

Shaping Athletes' Skills

One of your principal teaching duties is to reward positive effort or behavior—in terms of successful skill execution—when you see it. An athlete properly throws the shot put in practice, and you immediately say, "That's the way to follow through! Good throw!" This, plus a smile and a thumbs-up gesture, goes a long way toward reinforcing that technique in that athlete. However, sometimes you may have a long dry spell before you see correct techniques to reinforce. It's difficult to reward athletes when they don't execute skills correctly. How can you shape their skills if this is the case?

Shaping skills takes practice on your athletes' part and patience on yours. Expect your athletes to make errors. Telling the athlete who made the good throw that she did a good job doesn't ensure that she'll have the same success next time. Seeing inconsistency in your athletes' technique can be frustrating. It's even more challenging to stay positive when your athletes repeatedly perform a skill incorrectly or show a lack of enthusiasm for learning. It can certainly be frustrating to see athletes who seemingly don't heed your advice and continue to make the same mistakes.

Although it is normal to get frustrated sometimes when teaching skills, part of successful coaching is controlling this frustration. Instead of getting upset, use these six guidelines for shaping skills:

1. *Think small initially.*

   Reward the first signs of behavior that approximate what you want. Then reward closer and closer approximations of the desired behavior. In short, use your reward power to shape the behavior you seek.

2. *Break skills into small steps.*

   For instance, in learning proper sprint form, one of your athletes has good posture and leg action, but she swings her arms with a high, across-the-chest motion. Reinforce the correct techniques of posture and leg action, and teach her to run with her arms skimming her shorts. Once she masters this, you can focus on getting her to perfect the skill by driving her arms backward and allowing them to swing forward with a relaxed, elastic response.

3. *Develop one component of a skill at a time.*

   Don't try to shape two components of a skill at once. For example, in the throws, athletes must begin with a proper grip, get in a comfortable and appropriate stance, and use proper mechanics in executing the throw. Athletes should focus first on one aspect (grip), then on another (stance), and then the remaining components. Athletes who have problems mastering a skill are often trying to improve two or more components at once. You should help these athletes isolate a single component.

4. *Use reinforcement only occasionally, for the best examples.*

   By focusing only on the best examples, you will help athletes continue to improve once they've mastered the basics. Using occasional reinforcement during practice allows athletes to have more active time instead of having to constantly stop and listen to your instructions. Track and field skills are best learned through a lot of repetition, such as drills and competitive activities, and you should make the best use of team practice time by allowing the athletes to have as much training time as possible.

5. *Relax your reward standards.*

   As athletes learn a new skill or learn to combine two or more skills into one action, a temporary deterioration of previously learned skills may occur, and you may need to relax your expectations. For example, a shot-putter has learned how to throw the shot from a basic power stance and is now learning how to modify that technique to include a glide. While learning the new position and getting the rhythm down, the athlete's execution of both components may be poor. A similar degeneration of skills may occur during growth spurts while the coordination of muscles, tendons, and ligaments catches up to the growth of bones.

6. *Go back to the basics.*

If, however, a well-learned skill degenerates for long, you may need to restore it by going back to the basics. If necessary, have the athlete practice the skill using a low-pressure activity. For example, let a hurdler practice with a foam hurdle, adding a real hurdle only when the athlete is comfortable with his technique.

> **Coaching Tip**
> For older age groups or athletes with advanced skills, coaches can ask athletes to "self-coach." With the proper guidance and a positive team environment, young athletes can think about how they perform a skill and how they might be able to perform it better. Self-coaching is best done at practice, where an athlete can experiment with learning new skills.

Detecting and Correcting Errors

Good coaches recognize that athletes make two types of errors: learning errors and performance errors. Learning errors occur because athletes don't know how to perform a skill; that is, they have not yet developed the correct motor pattern in the brain to perform a particular skill. Performance errors are made not because athletes don't know how to execute the skill but because they have made a mistake in executing what they do know. There is no easy way to know whether an athlete is making learning or performance errors; part of the art of coaching is being able to sort out which type of error each mistake is.

The process of helping your athletes correct errors begins with observing and evaluating their performances to determine if the mistakes are learning or performance errors. Carefully watch your athletes to see if they routinely make the errors in both practice and competition settings or if the errors tend to occur only at meets. If the latter is the case, then your athletes are making performance errors. For performance errors, you need to look for the reasons your athletes are not performing as well as they can; perhaps they are nervous, or maybe they get distracted by the meet setting. If the mistakes are learning errors, then you need to help the athletes learn the skill, which is the focus of this section.

When correcting learning errors, there is no substitute for your own mastery of the skill. The better you understand a skill—not only how it is performed correctly but also what causes learning errors—the more helpful you will be in correcting your athletes' mistakes.

One of the most common coaching mistakes is providing inaccurate feedback and advice on how to correct errors. Don't rush into error correction; wrong feedback or poor advice will hurt the learning process more than no feedback or advice at all. If you are uncertain about the cause of the problem or how to correct it, you should continue to observe and analyze until you are more sure. As a rule, you should see the error repeated more than just occasionally before attempting to correct it.

Correct One Error at a Time

Suppose Megan, one of your more experienced sprinters, is having trouble with her block starts. She tends to position her hips too low in the "set" position and often takes her first step with the wrong foot. What do you do?

First, decide which error to correct first—athletes learn more effectively when they attempt to correct one error at a time. Determine whether one error is causing the other; if so, have the athlete correct that error first because it may eliminate the other error. In Megan's case, raising the hips might help her drive off the front pedal of the starting blocks. However, if neither error is causing the other, athletes should correct the error that is easiest to fix and that will bring the greatest improvement when remedied. For Megan, this probably means focusing on her first step to make sure that the back foot comes forward. You should explore whether the blocks are properly positioned to match Megan's natural leg dominance. Once you're sure of her block positioning and she is taking her first step with the correct foot, then she should work on raising her hips higher during the "set" command. Note that improvement in the first area may even motivate her to correct the other error.

Use Positive Feedback to Correct Errors

The positive approach to correcting errors includes emphasizing what to do instead of what not to do. Use praise, rewards, and encouragement to correct errors. Acknowledge correct performance as well as efforts to improve. By using positive feedback, you can help your athletes feel good about themselves and promote a strong desire to achieve.

When you're working with one athlete at a time, the positive approach to correcting errors includes four steps:

1. *Praise effort and correct performance.*

   Praise the athlete for trying to perform a skill correctly and for performing any parts of it correctly. Praise the athlete immediately after he performs the skill, if possible. Keep the praise simple: "Good try," "Way to hustle," "Good form," or "That's the way to follow through." You can also use nonverbal feedback, such as smiling, clapping your hands, or any facial or body expression that shows approval.

   Make sure you're sincere with your praise. Don't indicate that an athlete's effort was good when it wasn't. Usually an athlete knows when he has made a sincere effort to perform the skill correctly, and he will perceive undeserved praise for what it is—untruthful feedback to make him feel good. Likewise, don't indicate that an athlete's performance was correct when it wasn't.

2. *Give simple and precise feedback to correct errors.*

Don't burden an athlete with a long or detailed explanation of how to correct an error. Give just enough feedback so that the athlete can correct one error at a time. Before giving feedback, recognize that some athletes readily accept it immediately after the error; others will respond better if you slightly delay the correction.

For errors that are complicated to explain and difficult to correct, you should try the following:

- Explain and demonstrate what the athlete should have done. Do not demonstrate what the athlete did wrong.
- Explain the cause (or causes) of the error if it isn't obvious.
- Explain why you are recommending the correction you have selected if it's not obvious.

3. *Make sure the athlete understands your feedback.*

If the athlete doesn't understand your feedback, she won't be able to correct the error. Ask the athlete to repeat the feedback and to explain and demonstrate how it will be used. If the athlete can't do this, you should be patient and present your feedback again. Then have the athlete repeat the feedback after you're finished.

4. *Provide an environment that motivates the athlete to improve.*

Your athletes won't always be able to correct their errors immediately, even if they do understand your feedback. Encourage them to "hang tough" and stick with it when they seem discouraged or when corrections are difficult. For more difficult corrections, remind athletes that it will take time, and that the improvement will happen only if they work at it. Encourage those athletes with little self-confidence. Saying something like, "You were keeping your hips up really well today; with practice, you'll become more consistent with your timing and clear that height without a problem," can motivate an athlete to continue to refine her high jumping skills.

Other athletes may be very self-motivated and need little help from you in this area; with these athletes, you can practically ignore step 4 when correcting an error. Although motivation comes from within, you should try to provide an environment of positive instruction and encouragement to help your athletes improve.

A final note on correcting errors: Sports such as track and field provide unique challenges in this endeavor because you might be working with several athletes simultaneously. How do you provide individual feedback in a group setting using a positive approach? Instead of yelling (and embarrassing the athlete) during the middle of an activity, you should pull aside the athlete who is having trouble and then provide one-on-one feedback. This type of feedback has several advantages:

- The athlete will be more receptive to the one-on-one feedback.
- The other athletes are still active and still practicing skills, and they are unable to hear your discussion.
- Because the rest of the group is still practicing, you'll feel compelled to make your comments simple and concise—which is more helpful to the athlete.

This doesn't mean you can't use the group setting to give specific, positive feedback. You can do so to emphasize correct group and individual performances. Use this group feedback approach only for positive statements, though. Keep any negative feedback for individual discussions.

Dealing With Misbehavior

Young athletes will misbehave at times; it's only natural. Following are two ways you can respond to misbehavior: through extinction or discipline.

Track and Field No-Nos

It's inevitable that your athletes will violate minor rules during practices and meets. But you must make it clear to your athletes that some actions are unacceptable and can result in being removed from the practice, the meet, or even the team, depending on the severity of the infraction. Here are some examples:

- Throwing a relay baton intentionally in celebration or frustration
- Intentionally trying to interfere with another runner during a race by tripping or shoving
- Intentionally throwing an implement where it is not safe to do so
- Swearing, taunting an opponent, or arguing with an official

Your role as a coach is not limited to teaching fundamentals; you must also promote good sporting behavior both on and off the track or field. For example, encourage your athletes to wish other competitors well before a competition, to help the coaches put away the equipment after practice, and to offer support to teammates who are struggling to learn a complex new skill. Everyone involved with the team will appreciate this behavior.

Extinction

Ignoring a misbehavior—neither rewarding nor disciplining it—is called *extinction*. This can be effective under certain circumstances. In some situations, disciplining young people's misbehavior only encourages them to act up further because of the recognition they get. Ignoring misbehavior teaches youngsters that it is not worth your attention.

Sometimes, though, you cannot wait for a behavior to fizzle out. When an athlete causes danger to herself or others, or disrupts the activities of others, you need to take immediate action. Tell the offending athlete that the behavior must stop and that discipline will follow if it doesn't. If the athlete doesn't stop misbehaving after the warning, you should use discipline.

Extinction also doesn't work well when a misbehavior is self-rewarding. For example, you may be able to keep from grimacing if a youngster kicks you in the shin, but even so, the youngster still knows you were hurt. Therein lies the reward. In these circumstances, it is also necessary to discipline the athlete for the undesirable behavior.

Extinction works best in situations where athletes are seeking recognition through mischievous behaviors, clowning, or grandstanding. Usually, if you are patient, their failure to get your attention will cause the behavior to disappear. However, you must be alert that you don't extinguish desirable behavior. When youngsters do something well, they expect to be positively reinforced. Not rewarding them will likely cause them to discontinue the desired behavior.

> **Coaching Tip**
>
> Involve older athletes in the process of setting team rules and the consequences for breaking them. Athletes who are 12 or older are capable of brainstorming ideas about discipline for common situations such as being late for practice, criticizing another athlete, or talking back to the coach. Once you've agreed on a list of rules and consequences, each athlete should sign an agreement to cement her willingness to abide by them.

Discipline

Some educators say we should never discipline young people but should only reinforce their positive behaviors. They argue that discipline does not work, creates hostility, and sometimes develops avoidance behaviors that may be more unwholesome than the original problem behavior. It is true that discipline does not always work and that it can create problems when used ineffectively; however, when used appropriately, discipline is effective in eliminating undesirable behaviors without creating other undesirable consequences. You must use discipline because it is impossible to guide athletes through positive reinforcement and extinction alone. Discipline is part of the positive approach when these guidelines are followed:

- Discipline athletes in a corrective way to help them improve now and in the future. Never use discipline to retaliate or to make yourself feel better.

- Impose discipline in an impersonal way when athletes break team rules or otherwise misbehave. Shouting at or scolding athletes indicates that your attitude is one of revenge.
- Once a good rule has been agreed on, ensure that athletes who violate it experience the unpleasant consequences of their misbehavior. Don't wave discipline threateningly over their heads. Just do it, but warn an athlete once before disciplining.
- Be consistent in administering discipline.
- Don't discipline using consequences that may cause you guilt. If you can't think of an appropriate consequence right away, tell the athlete you will talk with him after you think about it. You might consider involving the athlete in designing a consequence.
- Once the discipline is completed, don't make athletes think that they are "in the doghouse." Always make them believe they're valued members of the team.
- Make sure that what you think is discipline isn't perceived by the athlete as a positive reinforcement; for instance, keeping an athlete out of doing a certain activity or portion of the training session may be just what the athlete wanted.
- Never discipline athletes for making mistakes when they are performing.
- Never use physical activity—running laps or doing push-ups—as discipline. To do so only causes athletes to resent physical activity, something we want them to learn to enjoy throughout their lives.
- Use discipline sparingly. Constant discipline and criticism causes athletes to turn their interests elsewhere and to resent you as well.

7

Coaching the Sprints, Hurdles, and Relays

The sprints, hurdles, and relays are the fastest events on the track. They are also typically the most popular events in track and field, with more athletes entered in these events than all the other events combined. The sprints are full-speed races over a short course—usually, events 400 meters and under are considered sprints. The hurdles are short races over barriers set at specific distances. The relays are contested by having four runners on each relay team, with each runner running one section of a determined course; teammates exchange a baton as they go.

From a developmental perspective, the popularity of the sprints is good because training for sprinting is fun and provides a set of fundamental skills that transfers well to other events and sports. Specifically, acceleration and the ability to move quickly can be developed by training for the speed events. These are valuable attributes for athletes in most team sports. However, there *is* a limit to how much full-speed running your athletes can do in one day, so you should make sure that they do not overrace. Although athletes may want to run several races in one meet, this is not good for long-term development, and it increases the risk of injury in the short term. Instead, your athletes should participate in two or three races per meet and should focus on developing their ability to coordinate the movements of full-speed running.

See table 7.1 for a list of the sprint, hurdle, and relay events for each age group for both the USATF Junior Olympics and the Hershey's Track & Field Games.

Table 7.1

USATF Junior Olympics	
Bantam (ages 10 and under)	100-meter dash, 200-meter dash, 400-meter dash, 4×100-meter relay, 4×400-meter relay
Midget (ages 11 and 12)	100-meter dash, 200-meter dash, 400-meter dash, 80-meter hurdles, 4×100-meter relay, 4×400-meter relay, 4×800-meter relay
Youth (ages 13 and 14)	100-meter dash, 200-meter dash, 400-meter dash, 100-meter hurdles, 200-meter hurdles, 4×100-meter relay, 4×400-meter relay, 4×800-meter relay
Intermediate (ages 15 and 16)	100-meter dash, 200-meter dash, 400-meter dash, 100-meter hurdles (girls) or 110-meter hurdles (boys), 400-meter hurdles, 4×100-meter relay, 4×400-meter relay, 4×800-meter relay
Young (ages 17 and 18)	100-meter dash, 200-meter dash, 400-meter dash, 100-meter hurdles (young women) or 110-meter hurdles (young men), 400-meter hurdles, 4×100-meter relay, 4×400-meter relay, 4×800-meter relay

Hershey's Track & Field Games	
Ages 9 and 10	50-meter dash, 100-meter dash, 200-meter dash, 400-meter dash, 4×100-meter relay
Ages 11 and 12	100-meter dash, 200-meter dash, 400-meter dash, 4×100-meter relay
Ages 13 and 14	100-meter dash, 200-meter dash, 4×100-meter relay

The Sprints

Although it seems simple enough to run from here to there as fast as you can, sprinting is considered a very complex task. Moving the legs and arms in a coordinated way to go full speed is very demanding. Many young athletes seem to be able to run all out over a short course without having to be taught the details of sprint mechanics. However, to reach full potential, develop consistency, and reduce the chance of injury, athletes need careful instruction and practice. To help your athletes stay healthy as they train to become fast, you need to understand the following aspects of sprinting: physiology and biomechanics of sprinting, the phases of a race, and sprinting form.

Physiological Principles of Sprinting

Physiology is the study of the body systems and parts. Learning some of the basics of physiology can be helpful for the coach working with sprinters. In this section, we consider how muscles work, look at the energy systems that fuel muscles, and examine how coaches can help athletes recruit more fast-twitch muscle fibers.

> **Coaching Tip**
>
> Of course, each athlete is unique and will run with his own style. The important thing is to contain these style elements within the boundaries of solid fundamental technique. The coach needs to discern what parts of the sprinter's style need to be improved and what parts can be allowed to stay the same. Developing the ability to discern this takes time, experience, and continued study of the sport. The general idea is to use coaching cues and drills to help athletes stay healthy and get faster.

Muscular Contraction

The mechanical process of moving the body happens through muscular contraction. Very simply, muscles shorten to cause limbs to move. When muscles on one side of the body shorten to create movement, muscles on the other side of the body must lengthen. Shortening a muscle is called a concentric contraction. Lengthening a muscle is called an eccentric contraction. For example, the muscles of the upper hamstring (the back of the upper leg) shorten to cause the leg to move back under the hips, while the muscles on the front of the leg relax to allow the movement. In sprinting, this muscle action is complicated because it all happens at full speed. Coordinating the rapid-fire eccentric and concentric contractions of muscles throughout the entire body in order to accelerate to maximum speed—and then maintain that speed—requires very specific practice.

Energy Systems

Exercise physiologists use the terms *aerobic* and *anaerobic* to describe how the body burns fuel for all human activity. The fuel that the body uses to create movement is called ATP (adenosine triphosphate), and a person can only store a limited amount of this fuel. After the supply of fuel is used, the person must replenish his stores to keep moving. When a person is moving with lower intensities, ATP is consumed and replenished in the presence of oxygen, and the person is using the aerobic (meaning, "with oxygen") energy system. This system is very efficient and enables a person to maintain movement for long periods. When a person is engaging in high-intensity activities, such as sprinting and hurdling, ATP is consumed and replenished without oxygen (anaerobic). During intense efforts that last longer than about seven seconds, this process creates metabolic waste known as lactic acid. Burning and resynthesizing ATP without oxygen is very inefficient, so high-intensity movement can only be tolerated for about a minute. After that, the body must use oxygen to continue moving, and true high intensity is not possible. So, learning to run economically is important.

The farther an athlete can get down the track before anaerobic energy gets replaced by aerobic, the better. One way to run more economically is to use elastic potential. Elastic potential is enhanced by maintaining posture and using stretch reflexes set up in the technique. Focusing on maintaining a smooth rhythm can also help an athlete run economically. Just as a car gets better gas mileage when driven smoothly at a consistent speed, the body can also work more efficiently at a steady pace.

Muscle Fibers and Motor Unit Recruitment

Technically speaking, muscle fibers are divided into three categories: Type I (slow-twitch) fibers create little force but have great endurance; type IIb (fast-twitch) fibers create great force for brief bursts of power; and type IIa fibers are in the middle because they have more endurance than type IIb fibers but cannot generate as much force. For sprinting and hurdling, the goal is to recruit as many fast-twitch muscle fibers as possible. Muscles can be trained to fire off in a certain order with a certain amount of force. Motor units are the nervous system switches that tell a group of muscle fibers to fire. The key is to program the motor units to coordinate in a pattern that maximizes performance. In this respect, here are a few things to remember when working with your sprinters:

1. Teach athletes to go full speed before they go full speed. A dose of full-speed running should be included at the end of a warm-up on meet days and quality practice days. You want the motor units to be recruited before the gun goes off.

2. Teach athletes that specificity of training is the key to creating a program of motor unit firing. This is why speed endurance work should be done very cautiously and only when a base of speed has been developed.

3. Teach athletes the proper mechanics of sprinting technique in all drills and workouts. Correct improper technique when you see it. Do not let bad habits become programs.

4. Teach athletes that type IIb (fast-twitch) fibers are only recruited during great force demand. Force demand can be increased by sprinting short distances at full speed and by running with a slight resistance.

Biomechanical Principles of Sprinting

Biomechanics is the study of how the body responds to the laws and principles of mechanics and physics. Concepts such as levers, gravity, Newton's laws, and so forth are used to learn how the body can be more effective. Here, we consider these three points: action and reaction, conservation of angular momentum, and the role of posture in creating a stretch reflex.

Action and Reaction

You may recall Newton's third law: For every action, there is an equal and opposite reaction. In sprinting, this fundamental concept can be used to make sure that a runner is focusing on the right technical points. What actions can sprinters perform that will cause the intended reaction of moving down the track? The main idea is to strike the track with the foot in a way that will propel the body toward the finish line as quickly as possible. This means two major things. First, the athlete must strike the track with the foot in a way that generates movement horizontally toward the finish line. Bouncing up and down is inefficient and slow. The second point is ground contact time. The quicker and more forcefully the sprinter strikes the track, the faster the return will be. Long, slow ground contacts cause slow running. Sprinting requires quick and powerful foot contacts.

Conservation of Angular Momentum

A short limb moves faster than a long limb, but a long limb can generate more force. This trade-off, known as conservation of angular momentum, comes into play in sprinting in two major ways—heel recovery and developmental considerations.

A sprinter needs to make the leg as short as possible as it swings forward (this part of the running stroke is known as heel recovery). Lifting the heel to the top of the hamstring immediately following the active backward contact stroke shortens the lever of the free leg and creates faster return. Also, when the lower leg is tucked close to the thigh during the recovery phase, strain on the hamstring is reduced. A low heel recovery creates a long and slow lever that the hamstring has to control to keep the knee from overextending. In other words, because the lever is long, it can produce more force, and the hamstring has to work hard to decelerate the lower leg. Proper heel recovery is more efficient and reduces the chance of injury.

Regarding development, you must understand that children might not have the muscular strength to hold their arms in a disciplined form. The limbs, especially the arms, form long levers that may be creating greater force than the athlete can control. Some athletes regulate this by folding their arms tightly at the elbows to create very short arm levers. This solution may stop the coach from nagging about waving arms, but it is not proper technique. Learning to control the arms is important, but it must be addressed through general strength development, as well as patient teaching of proper technique.

Posture and Stretch Reflex

Connective tissue has elastic qualities, and recruiting this elastic potential makes sprinting more efficient. Elasticity is increased by holding proper posture. To maintain proper posture, athletes must learn that the hips need to be held in a slightly "tucked" position during all phases of the sprint races. Tucked hip posture is efficient because it sets up a stretch reflex of the connective tissue on the front of the hips and legs. This tissue acts like rubber bands and pulls the leg back in front of the body. Think of this elastic response as "free energy" that dramatically improves running economy. Failure to hold the hips in the proper position shortens the length of the stretch in the front of the body and reduces the elastic response. Furthermore, when poor hip posture shortens the stretch in the front of the body, it lengthens the stretch in the back of the body. This causes the hamstring to do more work and exposes it to ranges of motion that can be risky, especially in states of fatigue.

The shoulder girdle also uses a stretch reflex in sprinting. The active phase of the arm action is when the arm moves aggressively backward. As the arm moves back, the elbow opens slightly to elongate the lever and create a bit more force. The arm should go to the end of the range of motion (elbow about as high as the shoulder) and create a stretch of the shoulder's connective tissue. The arm closes a bit at the elbow as the arm returns in an elastic reflex.

The Three Phases of Sprinting

The sprints—whether it's the actual sprints, the hurdles, or the relays—are broken down into three phases: acceleration, full-speed running, and running fast in a state of fatigue.

As a coach, you will want to teach these phases in the order they occur. In other words, athletes must first learn how to get up to full speed. Then they can practice running high-quality efforts at full speed, including using proper technique at maximum velocity. Finally, they can work on maintaining fast running while fatigued. Too often, coaches put together training programs in the opposite order. Starting the season with speed endurance work when a solid base of speed has not been established is a quick route to plateaus, frustration, and injury. If an athlete is not going fast during a set of repeats, especially near the finish line, the athlete is not really training for the sprints.

Acceleration

The object is to transition from a still position to full-speed running as quickly and efficiently as possible. The athlete should use a forward lean (see figure 7.1a) when accelerating from a still position. However, this must not be over-

a   b

Figure 7.1   Acceleration for the sprints: *(a)* correct and *(b)* incorrect.

exaggerated. The athlete needs to get all available power out of the hips and legs during each acceleration stroke. Breaking at the hips (see figure 7.1*b*) can happen when athletes are trying to stay lower than their strength levels will support. When children without experience and strength attempt to imitate this low get-out, they often bend at the waist. This bent-over posture leaves stored energy in the hips and exposes the hamstring for potential injury.

An important characteristic of acceleration is that the foot makes contact with the track below the hips or even slightly behind. The leg action is then a pushing action down the track. During the first few acceleration steps, these pushes should be complete and strong. Complete, big pushes may appear to be slower because there will be increased ground contact time. An incorrect response to this is to try to move the feet faster without as much movement (also known as displacement) toward the finish line. Imagine the cartoon characters Speedy Gonzalez and Fred Flintstone spinning their feet in place in a cloud of dust before they actually take off running. Acceleration is pushing the body down the track, not spinning wheels.

The arm action during acceleration is very important (see figure 7.2). Big, strong, and complete movements of the upper body are essential to build up momentum. In all phases of sprinting, the backward stroke of the arm is the active phase. Therefore, the sprinter should be cued to drive the

Figure 7.2   Arm action when accelerating.

elbows back. The return to the front happens naturally with a stretch reflex at the shoulder. On the backward phase, the elbows should get as high as the shoulder. In the front, the hands should get no higher than the chin. It is okay to have an opening and closing at the elbow joint. Locking the elbow in a certain position is not advised.

Stride lengths gradually increase throughout the acceleration phase. At the point when they become consistently the same length, the majority of acceleration is over, and the athlete is approaching full-speed running.

Full-Speed Running

The forward lean becomes less noticeable as athletes approach maximum velocity, or full speed. The proper posture at peak speed is often described as "tall." The lean is gone, and runners maintain a fully upright position (see figure 7.3). Note that athletes with a background in team field sports such as soccer and football sometimes have difficulty with this tall position. Lowering the hips is an essential technique for field sports because quick changes in direction are part of the game. Unlike field sports, there is no need to change directions in the sprint races. Athletes can commit to moving forward at full speed. Running tall lengthens the levers and improves efficiency.

At full speed, athletes must maintain a consistent tempo. This rhythm is established by finding the right balance of stride length and stride frequency. Rhythm endurance is the ability to maintain optimal stride frequency over time. Teach athletes that abruptly "changing gears" late in a race—in other words, trying to reaccelerate—is dangerous because it puts enormous strain on the hamstrings. Instead, sprinters should concentrate on maintaining a smooth cadence.

Minimizing ground contact time during this phase is very important. Preflexing the feet (dorsiflexing) helps facilitate fast ground contact because less time is spent stabilizing. The foot makes contact with the track slightly in front of the body, and the locomotive action is a pull with the posterior chain (glutes and hamstrings). As soon as the body has passed over the base of support, the heel is brought quickly up, making the lever of the free leg as short as possible for the recovery swing back to the front. Spending too much time with the leg on the

Figure 7.3   Body positioning for full-speed running.

backside is a common error. Proper hip posture helps create an elastic response at the hip for this action.

Running Fast in a State of Fatigue

In teaching children to sprint when they are tired, two important things should be considered. First, if their technique changes (e.g., tightening up, low knee lift, low heel recovery), they may be more at risk of injury and disappointing performances. Second, not concentrating during hard workouts and competition could cause the development of poor habits such as bad posture, tightness, and erratic and slow turnover. These habits are difficult to break.

> **Coaching Tip**
> Staying loose is essential in the last part of the race. Sprinters should try to stay loose using discipline, focus, and techniques such as pumping the arms. Tightness often starts in the face. Encourage runners to keep their face and neck muscles loose. The goal is to stay as loose as possible without allowing posture to deteriorate.

Be careful not to let athletes overstride. At track meets, as athletes approach the finish line in a long sprint race, you may often hear coaches and parents yell from the stands, "Stride out!" This is a common misconception. In fact, artificially lengthening the stride in a state of deep fatigue can be dangerous. Correct form involves a fast stride frequency, quick ground reaction time, and slightly shorter strides. Overstriding causes longer ground contact times, leads to a braking action, and puts tremendous pressure on the already stressed posterior chain. Quick ground contact times are essential in the last two phases of the sprint race. Just as a child would put her foot out in front of her to stop or slow down a tricycle, the term *braking action* means that as the runner casts her lower leg out in front of the body to elongate the stride, that leg acts like a brake. Rather, the athlete should try to keep the legs under the hips (see figure 7.4). The key is to maintain a fast stride frequency. In many cases, the stride length in the final part of a long sprint will actually be a bit shorter.

Athletes can focus on aggressively driving their elbows back and having powerful, complete movements in the upper body. Pumping the arms through a complete range of motion can help keep the upper body from tightening up.

Figure 7.4 Leg movement when in a state of fatigue.

Sprinting Form

When teaching your athletes proper sprinting form, you should focus on these parts of the sprint stroke: posture and looseness, stride length and frequency, ground contact, free leg recovery, and arm action. Note that the following points apply to all phases of sprinting, unless stated otherwise.

Posture and Looseness

Two important aspects of sprinting are posture and looseness. Poor posture forces the body to fire off muscles inefficiently to stabilize itself rather than move down the track. Tight muscles restrict full-speed contractions. Athletes must maintain good posture and overall looseness while moving as fast as possible down the track.

Proper posture requires the sprinter to stay tall, with the lower part of the hips rotated slightly forward and the feet dorsiflexed (as shown previously in figure 7.3 on page 74). Another critical part of posture is the position of the head. Keeping the head in a neutral position relative to the spine is important for efficiency and injury prevention. Runners whipping their head from side to side in the home stretch of a 400-meter race may assume that this display of effort is helpful. Coaches need to teach that straining and whipping the head does not make athletes run faster. As much as possible, runners should allow the skeletal system to support the head. In other words, the head should remain directly above the shoulders while keeping the neck straight. Deviating from this posture causes the muscles of the neck and trunk to expend more energy in supporting the head, and this reduces the efficiency of the runner.

Of course, if a runner is too loose, it might be difficult to maintain proper posture, so the key is to find a balance. The athlete must be loose from the face through the hips (being careful not to let the feet get floppy). Excessive tightness in the face, neck, or upper body will restrict the ability of the hips and legs to move at maximum speed. Looseness should also be demonstrated in the hips. While the chest stays perpendicular to the direction of running, the hips should be loose and move in subtle oscillations. Freezing the hips and lifting from the crease at the upper leg is a common mistake made by young runners.

Stride Length and Stride Frequency

Stride length and stride frequency are two measurable aspects of the sprint that can be used to mathematically calculate speed. Obviously, longer strides and a greater rate of turnover will make a runner go faster. As discussed previously in regard to running fast when fatigued, elongating the stride by casting out the lower leg in front of the body can be dangerous. Stride length should be increased by aggressively pushing the body forward with the leg that is on the track, not by reaching with the free leg. Athletes must also make sure that these pushes are mostly toward the finish line; driving up instead of out causes runners to be too bouncy. Going up and down rather than straight ahead wastes time and energy.

The best adult sprinters have stride lengths no longer than one and one-third of their body height (measured in competition at the highest levels)—this length, remember, needs to be created by aggressive push-offs, not reaches. Almost no research has been done on children, but we can assume that the adult number (one and one-third of body height) should be the maximum for elite youth. For developing youth, using shorter and quicker strides will help sprinters stay healthy and develop their nervous system for long-term success. As they grow and get stronger, stride length will increase.

Ground Contact

The ball of the foot should make contact with the track slightly in front of the body. Again, making contact too far in front causes a braking action. The foot must be flexed toward the knee during all phases except the final push-off. Having a preflexed foot at the point of ground contact conserves energy and allows the runner to concentrate on moving horizontally down the track, rather than stabilizing first and then moving toward the finish. When the foot lands with a pointy or dangling toe, the body is forced to find stability and balance before it can apply force.

Free Leg Recovery

When there is a problem with this part of the running cycle (i.e., free leg recovery), it is sometimes referred to as poor backside mechanics. The most common problem is when the leg cycles up and back after the final push-off from the track. Sprinters must understand that stride length should be created by a forceful push-off from the track, not a long and passive float phase.

Typically, poor free leg recovery is caused by weak hips. The consequence of this is a passive push off the track, low knee lift, and excess strain on the posterior chain. Throughout the race, shortening the free leg as much as possible promotes efficiency and speed. The exception to this is the first step from the starting position. Many athletes demonstrate low heel recovery in the first step. This is acceptable because long levers—although slower—generate more force, and the goal of acceleration is to overcome the static position with powerful strokes.

Arm Action

The elbow joint opens and closes in a coordinated movement with the opposite leg. As the body passes over the foot that is on the ground, the leg in contact is relatively straight. At this point, the opposite arm is also swinging close to the hips and demonstrates less bend.

Starts for the Sprints

Because the overall time it takes to complete a sprint race is relatively short, effective starting technique is very important. Reaction time and acceleration are fundamental to sprinting success. Athletes need to know how to get up to full speed quickly and efficiently using the mechanics of acceleration. Therefore, you should teach acceleration early and often. Starting techniques can be broken into two general categories: standing starts and block starts.

Standing Starts

In the Hershey program, starting blocks are not permitted, which makes the Hershey program accessible to children without the specialized training and equipment. For this reason, learning how to do standing starts is clearly important for children participating in this program. Standing starts are also an important training tool for all sprinters and a good starting technique for children without the strength to come out of a low three- or four-point stance.

For a standing start, you first need to help the athlete determine which leg goes forward and which leg goes back. Most athletes have one side of their body that is relatively strong and one side that is quick. Typically, for a standing start, the strong leg goes forward and the quick leg goes back. Two techniques can be used to help athletes determine their strong side and their quick side for standing starts:

1. Athletes run up and kick a soccer ball (or you may simply ask them which leg they kick with). One side will brace while the other leg swings through and kicks the ball. The kicking leg is often the quick leg.

2. Athletes stand tall and fall forward. The leg that naturally swings forward to catch the fall is the quick leg and would go in the back position.

Once the front foot is established, learning the basic fundamentals of the standing start is quite intuitive for most children. At the starting line, the front foot faces the running direction without any part of the foot actually touching the line (see figure 7.5). The back foot can face the same direction, or athletes can open their stance slightly for more traction. Body weight should be distributed with slightly more pressure on the front leg. A slight bend is maintained at the ankles, knees, and hips. The eyes are focused ahead on a position about 10 to 20 meters down the track.

The arms are positioned opposite the feet—that is, if the left foot is toeing the line, the right arm will be held forward. The hands should be held in loose fists or gently closed. Making tight fists is a common mistake that causes rigidity in the upper body and interferes with the stretch reflex of the shoulders. The starting command initiates an alternate arm action and a strong push off of the front foot. Alternate arm action means that as the quick leg moves forward, the arm on that side aggressively drives back.

Sprinters need to completely extend off the front foot, getting power from the hips, knees, ankle, and toes. At the completion of the push off the front foot, the body should be straight like an arrow from the foot to the top of the head.

Figure 7.5 Initial body positioning for the standing start.

Block Starts

Teaching the block start should be a natural progression from the standing start. You will want to begin teaching children starts using the standing start, but as children get stronger and more explosive, you can begin teaching the block start.

For the block start (see figure 7.6), the athlete's arms are fully locked out and perpendicular to the track. The hands are held in a slight bridge with the thumbs pointing in. The thumbs and the index fingers are near, but not touching, the starting line. The head, neck, and spine are held in a straight position. Tucking the chin or looking up disrupts this alignment. In the "set" position, the hips will be slightly higher than the head. The front leg is bent at the knee at about 90 degrees. The back leg is bent at the knee at about 135 degrees. The balls of both feet should be pressed against the blocks with a small part of the toes on the track. The heels are pressed slightly back.

Figure 7.6 Initial body positioning for the block start.

(continued)

On command, the athletes must come to the "take your mark" position (see figure 7.7). In this position, the feet and hands are in place, but the hips are lowered, and the athlete rests on the knee of the leg in the back block. In this position, the athlete must be very still. Once all the athletes are ready, the starter will call "set." The athlete must bring the hips up into the final starting position and again be very still. Once the children are set, the next sound is the signal to start.

Figure 7.7   "Take your mark" position for the block start.

To determine how the blocks will be set, athletes must first establish the desired start position. Have your athletes practice getting into the proper position at the starting line without blocks. For beginners, this will take quite a bit of adjustment with the help of the coach. Once the proper posture (as previously outlined) is established, mark the position of the feet with chalk or tape and then set the blocks. Have the children measure how far each block is from the starting line using their own feet or a tape measure. For many runners, the front block will be placed one and three-quarters of their foot length from the starting line, and the back block will be placed about two and three-quarters of their foot length from the line.

Once the "set" position and the block placements are established, athletes should practice getting into that position with the rhythm of the starter's commands. Children need to practice setting their own blocks, holding still in the "marks" position, and coming to the "set" position and holding still. And, of course, they must practice reacting to the start command and accelerating toward the finish line.

To achieve effective block clearance at the start command, athletes must demonstrate the same movements described for the standing start: aggressive alternate arm action, a big push off the front foot, and complete application of force through all potential joints.

Sprinting Activities

The neuromuscular demand for running at full speed is great, so coaches must carefully select activities to train athletes for the sprints, hurdles, and relays. Training needs to be general in regard to the development of the whole athlete (posture, flexibility, stability, endurance and general strength) and specific in regard to the demands that are placed on the nervous and energy systems when sprinting. To meet this specific demand, some of the training must be done at very high intensity. As it is difficult to simulate the arousal levels of competition, it is suggested that training that is intended to happen at high intensity is done at least 95 percent. Other workouts are designed to build endurance and work on technique, so this type of training is often done at 75 percent. An easy trick to find 75 percent intensity is to have an athlete run three-quarters of a race distance and try to hit his or her full distance personal record (PR). For example, a Bantam girl might have a PR in the 100 meter of 15 seconds, so for technical rhythm runs, she could run 75 meters in that time. Here we describe three categories of activities that are important for the development of the young sprinter: locomotive moves, sprint-specific training, and stabilization work.

Locomotive Moves

The locomotive moves provided here are general sprinting activities that can serve three purposes. First, these moves put the athletes through controlled and event-specific range of motion. Therefore, these activities can be used by all members of a team as part of a group warm-up. Throwers, distance runners, and jumpers—in addition to the sprinters—will benefit from these fundamental locomotive moves. Second, these activities help athletes develop an understanding of the terminology you use to describe sprinting to better recognize proper mechanics and they help athletes gain a familiarity with the coaching cues used to correct technical faults. And third, these running activities will help athletes build the specific strength and flexibility needed to be able to execute proper sprinting form.

Note that locomotive moves can be done in lines or in a circle. Often, coaches set cones at approximately 10 to 15 meters apart on the track or on a grass field and athletes perform the moves in a line. Or, athletes can form a big circle with the coach in the middle. The coach leads the activities as athletes perform the moves while moving around in a circle.

MUMMY WALKS

This drill is a dynamic warm-up for the posterior chain (especially the hamstrings) and enables athletes to work on balance and lower leg stability. The athletes simply walk forward with the arms stretched out in front of them (like zombies or mummies). The legs are kept relatively straight and alternately swing forward at least as high as the navel. On one set, have the athletes keep the planted foot flat on the track throughout the entire swing to increase the demand and the stretch. On the second set, have the athletes bridge up onto the toes at the top of the swing.

KNEE HUGS

This drill is another dynamic warm-up for the posterior chain (especially the hamstrings) that enables athletes to work on balance and lower leg stability. Athletes move at a slow marching tempo, alternately hugging each knee to the chest. Essentially, this drill is similar to the A drill from the ABCs of Sprinting described on page 87, but at the top of the knee movement, the athlete grasps the leg and holds it in a stretch for two to four seconds while balancing on the other leg.

SHAG JOG

This drill is used as a general warm-up. The athletes jog (usually on grass) as slowly as possible, keeping the body very loose while not allowing posture to deteriorate.

ANKLE POPS

Some coaches call this drill "drum major" as the move resembles the straight leg prance of the leader of a marching band. This drill helps athletes practice fast ground contact made with the ball of the foot. With relatively straight legs, the athletes pop their feet off the track, moving the leg up and forward with no leg-shortening recovery phase.

TOE WALKS

This drill is used for strengthening the foot and lower leg. First, athletes walk on tiptoes with the feet facing forward, then on tiptoes with feet facing in, and finally on the toes with feet facing out. Athletes should then repeat the series while walking only on the heels, holding the toes off the track.

WALKING LUNGES

This drill stretches and strengthens the posterior chain and hip flexors. Athletes reach out with the front leg and stride into a lunge (the shin of the front leg is positioned perpendicular to the track). Athletes hold the trunk in an upright position, avoiding the tendency to lean into the front leg. Keeping the shin at a right angle to the track, the athlete lifts up over the front leg and lunges out into the next step.

SKIP TWISTS

This drill helps loosen and strengthen the hips and the trunk. Athletes skip forward with high knees while twisting the upper body in the direction opposite from the leg that is up. For example, when the right knee is forward, the athlete rotates the trunk so that the left elbow is twisted to the right. In other words, the athlete exaggerates the twisting of the trunk while maintaining the natural alternating action of the arms and legs.

LATERAL MOVES

This drill is done laterally, or side to side, to strengthen the lower leg, knees, and hips. Many children will have done this type of work in team sports; in that setting, children are usually coached to stay low throughout the move. However, for sprinting in track and field, you need to reinforce the characteristic of tall posture during all activities. Here are two classic lateral moves to add to your program:

- *Carioca.* Facing sideways, the athlete alternately sweeps the back leg in front and behind the leg facing the direction of movement.
- *Sideways skips.* The athletes face sideways and skip with big sweeping arm movements. The big rotational movements of the arms help develop flexibility and strength at the shoulder joint. During the sideways skip, the legs do not cross as in the carioca. The feet come together in the air, and the back leg pushes laterally during support.

Sprint-Specific Training

Sprint-specific training is what most people consider sprint training to be—running. As a coach, you should have a specific goal in mind when designing sprint-specific training workouts. Designing workouts that are "hard" is rarely a good approach, but, rather, your goal should be about specific preparation for the competitive task. To help align workouts with appropriate training goals, four categories of workouts can be considered: acceleration, maximum velocity, speed endurance, and rhythm work.

ACCELERATION

Acceleration training helps develop the start for the sprints. Beginners can practice a variety of starting positions to develop the hip strength needed to accelerate the body quickly. Some examples are starts from a three-point stance (one hand touching the ground), double leg jumps for distance into an acceleration run, resisted starts (coach holds the athletes hips back with a towel as the athlete works to accelerate), and practicing the competitive start (crouch for Hershey's program and blocks starts for more advanced athletes competing in the USATF Junior Olympics program). Consider the following volume ranges and examples for determining acceleration workouts.

- *Novice.* Maximum volume should not exceed 200 total meters. For example, a high-end goal workout would be 20 repeats of 10-meter multistarts (left hand down, right hand down, crouch with left foot forward, crouch with right foot forward, both hands down, where the circuit is repeated four times) at greater than 95 percent effort.
- *Intermediate.* Maximum volume should not exceed 250 total meters. For example, a high-end goal workout would be 25 repeats of 10-meter resisted starts at greater than 95 percent effort.
- *Advanced.* Maximum volume should not exceed 300 total meters. For example, a high-end goal workout would be 20 repeats of 15-meter competitive start rehearsals at greater than 95 percent effort.

MAXIMUM VELOCITY

Maximum velocity training is designed to develop running at full speed. After approximately 7 or 8 seconds of full-speed running, almost all athletes begin to slow down, so the active bouts of full-speed running for this type of training must be short and intense.

Coaches may choose to combine maximum velocity workouts with acceleration, as discussed previously. This means that athletes would continue to run at greater than 95 percent intensity after they have completed acceleration. In other cases, coaches may choose not to combine this with the acceleration component and focus only on maximum velocity by creating what is called a "fly zone" when using these workouts. The fly zone is made by setting 2 cones 15 to 30 meters apart on the track and athletes use a slower, gradual acceleration phase, only reaching full speed as they enter the zone. Consider the following volume ranges and examples for determining maximum velocity workouts.

- *Novice.* Maximum volume should not exceed 200 total meters. For example, a high-end goal workout would be 10 repeats of 20-meter miniraces.
- *Intermediate.* Maximum volume should not exceed 250 total meters. For example, a high-end goal workout would be 10 repeats of flying 25 meters at greater than 95 percent effort.
- *Advanced.* Maximum volume should not exceed 300 total meters. For example, a high-end goal workout would be relay exchange rehearsals at greater than 95 percent effort.

SPEED ENDURANCE

Speed endurance training (sometimes called "intensive tempo") is advanced training that develops your athletes' ability to run fast over distance. Typically, these bouts of running last anywhere between 20 seconds and one minute. For youth athletes, one speed endurance workout per week (or even every other week) plus a weekly competition is enough. Speed endurance work has a great metabolic demand, so the body must work very hard to provide anaerobic energy to maintain high speeds. As such, long recovery periods between intervals and sessions are required. One key coaching point here is to make sure that athletes are still running fast toward the end of the interval. Slow running, poor posture, long ground contact times, and excessive strain in the face and neck are all red flags that the workout is too much for the developmental level of the athlete. Create workouts that challenge athletes, but allow them to still be moving fast at the finish line. Be patient as athletes develop the ability to go farther without experiencing so much distress that they dramatically slow down. Consider the following volume ranges and examples for determining speed endurance workouts.

- *Novice.* Maximum volume should not exceed 500 total meters. For example, a high-end goal workout would be 3 repeats of 150 meters at greater than 90 percent with full recovery.
- *Intermediate.* Maximum volume should not exceed 700 total meters. For example, a high-end goal workout would be 3 repeats of 200 meters at greater than 90 percent with full recovery.
- *Advanced.* Maximum volume should not exceed 900 meters. For example, a high-end goal workout would be 3 repeats of 300 meters at greater than 90 percent with full recovery.

RHYTHM WORK

Rhythm work training (sometimes called "extensive tempo") develops athletes' ability to run at a controlled pace with proper sprint form over distance and can help athletes develop endurance and technique. Generally, this type of work is done at about 75 percent effort and these bouts of running last anywhere between 20 and 90 seconds. For these workouts, the focus should be on running loose and elastic with good posture, proper form, and quick turnover. Indeed, the turnover should be very similar to the competitive rate, but as the athlete is only going three-quarters speed (75 percent), stride length must be reduced. Consider the following volume ranges and examples for determining rhythm work workouts.

- *Novice.* Maximum volume should not exceed 600 total meters. For example, a high-end goal workout would be 8 repeats of 75 meters at 75 percent.
- *Intermediate.* Maximum volume should not exceed 900 total meters. For example, a high-end goal workout would be 4 repeats of 150 and 4 repeats of 75 meters, both at 75 percent.

- *Advanced.* Maximum volume should not exceed 1100 total meters. For example, a high-end goal workout would be 7 repeats of 150 meters at 75 percent.

Stabilization Work

A significant amount of training should be devoted to stabilizing your athletes' lower legs and hips. Just as a car will not go fast with bad tires or a weak suspension, neither will a runner without strong feet and ankles and stable hips. The following stabilization activities can be used during warm ups and cool downs at practices or coaches can use stabilization activities on recovery days when running is not the major focus of the day.

Note that in addition to the three activities provided here, the Hurdle Mobility activity described later in this chapter on page 90 can also be used with your sprinters and can serve as a cool-down activity after a challenging running workout. For sprinters, the Hurdle Mobility activity strengthens the hips and provides opportunities to work the hips over a large range of motion.

DYNAMIC RANGE OF MOTION

This drill involves a large, swinging movement of the limbs and is often used as a part of the warm-up for acceleration or maximum velocity workouts. The arms are whipped in large arcs forward and backward. Athletes can stand near a wall, a hurdle, or a fence to help balance themselves as the legs are whipped forward and backward over a large range of motion. Athletes perform two to three sets of ten for each exercise.

BALANCE WORK

This drill begins with athletes standing on one foot while maintaining good hip posture and dorsiflexing the foot that is in the air. A number of different moves can be done from this position: toe circles, leg swings, touching the toes, throwing medicine balls, upward reaching, trunk twists, etc. The training occurs when the leg that is on the ground flexes quickly to maintain balance as the athlete goes through various moves. This activity can be set up based on time or using a predetermined number of sets and reps.

TRUNK DEVELOPMENT

Any move that is designed to strengthen the trunk or core would fit into this category. Typical sit-ups or crunches or more advanced moves with exercise balls or other apparatus are all effective in developing the core. The body adapts very quickly to trunk development work, so this type of training activity can be done quite frequently including daily for more advanced athletes.

The ABCs of Sprinting

The following three drills are such a fundamental and common part of the sprinter's training program that they have come to be known as the ABCs of sprinting. These drills are typically performed in lines with cones set up 10 to 20 meters apart to form the start and finish lines. Begin by having the athletes go through the moves while marching, then gradually increase the tempo. For example, athletes march the first set, move at medium speed the second set, and move at close to full speed the third set. In addition, you can occasionally add a balance challenge by including a "freeze" command. As the athletes are doing the drill, the coach says "freeze," and the athletes try to stop where they are and balance on one foot while holding the proper sprint form.

A Drill

For this drill, the athletes bring the knee up to hip height or slightly higher as they move forward. The foot stays dorsiflexed. The athletes need to use proper hip posture, good arm action, and an overall tall posture (there should be no bending at the waist). The tempo and amplitude of the arm action should be coordinated with the lower body. The focus of the move is quick ground reaction time off the track. Athletes should focus on driving the knees up and down, not on moving toward the finish line. Sometimes the coach might have to walk slowly backward in front of the athletes to keep them from going too fast. After 10 to 15 meters, the coach can signal the athletes to break free and run it out a few steps.

B Drill

For this drill, the athletes perform the high knee movements as described for the A drill, but when the knee reaches hip height, the athlete extends the lower leg. This drill puts demand on the hamstring and serves as a dynamic warm-up and hamstring strengthener.

C Drill

For this drill, the athletes bring the knee up about half as high as in the A or B drill. In this drill, the athletes work on making the leg as short as possible—as quickly as possible—without disrupting hip posture.

Hurdles

Simply stated, hurdle events are sprints over barriers. The object is to clear the barrier as quickly, efficiently, and safely as possible and to sprint between the barriers in a way that sets up an effective takeoff position for the next hurdle. Clearing the barrier obviously adds an increased technical demand to the events; however, you should remember that these events are, in fact, sprints. Although not every great sprinter can hurdle, most great hurdlers are very good sprinters.

Training athletes for these events takes great patience and an enormous amount of teaching. Coaches need to be careful to set up a developmental training program that puts athletes in the position where they can successfully do the event in competition. The hurdles are not to be approached casually. Do not have athletes attempt competitive hurdling until they have completed a period of disciplined training and have demonstrated technical proficiency and consistency.

In addition, the athletes' safety while hurdling is a big concern for coaches. Setting up high wooden and metal barriers on the track and having young people "try" the event is absolutely not the way to go. Instead, you should use developmentally appropriate activities involving small barriers—such as yardsticks, pizza boxes, or commercially available minihurdles—to introduce hurdling to your athletes. These activities can be a fun way for an entire team to work on fitness, agility, and running technique. By observing these safer activities, you can identify athletes who appear to have potential to be successful in the competitive event. These athletes can then move on to more advanced work.

Hurdling Technique

Although several technical aspects of hurdling are common in all successful hurdlers, there is also a certain amount of variability. Some athletes dip their upper body aggressively as they go over the hurdle, while others appear to maintain an upright posture. Some athletes slam the lead leg down very close to the hurdle; others float over the hurdle and spend a significant amount of time in the air. With all this variation, how do coaches and athletes decide what is right? It starts with a basic understanding of the fundamentals. Then athletes and coaches have to make decisions about technique and style to work toward the best result.

Athletes first need to learn about the hurdling strides. There are two categories of races for hurdlers to consider when learning about the strides: hurdle races on the straightaway and hurdle races around the track. For the hurdle races that are on the straightaway (80 m, 100 m, and 110 m), athletes usually take either three, four, or five strides between the hurdles. Strides here represent the distance between foot contacts. So, for a 3-stride hurdler, there will actually be four foot contacts. More advanced athletes who develop the ability to use three strides between the hurdles will normally have the best results. Younger and shorter children will need to take four of five strides between the hurdles. For hurdle races around the track (200 m, 300 m, and 400 m), the barriers are set significantly farther apart and athletes will have to take many strides between each hurdle. There is a wide variation in the number of strides a hurdler will take between hurdles in these races. Beginners may take as many as 20 strides and advanced athletes may take only 13 strides. This becomes more complicated for beginners, because the number of strides between barriers will change during the course of the competition based on race conditions and fatigue. Because of these variables, hurdlers need to learn how to clear the barrier using either leg as the lead.

Regardless of the number of strides between hurdles, the lead-leg action begins with a drive of the lead knee toward the barrier. It is a common mistake for beginners to swing the leg toward the barrier with the foot in the lead and very little bend at the knee. Correct lead-leg action is a knee drive toward the hurdle and the knee joint will open up in flight.

Athletes must understand that the trail leg over the hurdle is also the takeoff leg in the hurdling action. Therefore, they need to have an aggressive push-off with the trail leg. A strong and complete push-off makes the movement faster and sets up a stretch reflex to get the leg into position and get it over the barrier. At takeoff, the lead knee and hip need to be aggressively displaced toward the hurdle. When moving over the hurdle, athletes must have a tight heel recovery in which the trail leg is shortened at the knee to speed up the movement over the barrier (see figure 7.8). In flight, the lead leg will be relatively linear, with the knee joint opening up and the lead leg becoming straighter during clearance. This does not mean that the leg is fully extended at the knee joint. Rather, the foot, knee, and leg should be moving directly forward and should not whip out to the side.

The arms and legs work together to create balance—when the left leg goes forward, the right arm naturally goes forward. The range of motion that the arms go through varies depending on the action of the legs. In hurdling, when the lead leg extends to clear the hurdle, the opposite arm generally extends too. Similarly, when the trail leg shortens with heel recovery, the opposite arm shortens.

On landing, the hurdler needs to resume fast running as early as possible. Developing control and balance allows this to happen. The athlete must try to get the hips back into position at the point of landing. Landing with a bend at the hips causes energy to be wasted in stabilization.

Figure 7.8   Positioning of the legs as the athlete moves over the hurdle.

Hurdling Activities

The following activities represent a few of the many drills that can be used to teach hurdling. Remember that practice for beginners should not simply be running over the hurdles set at the competitive height. Hurdling is dangerous and athletes need to develop a strong proficiency of the fundamental skills before rehearsing the competitive form. Practice should be comprised of selected drills that will help athletes gain mastery of technique.

HURDLE MOBILITY

Set up four to seven hurdles in a line so that the barriers are parallel and are butted against each other (the lower base of the hurdles are in contact with each other). The hurdles should be set at a height that allows the athletes to stand astride the barrier while standing on their toes. If you have more than six athletes, set up two or more stations so that the time waiting in line is minimized. During the drill, use coaching cues to reinforce the principles of effective hurdling, such as maintaining posture at all times and maintaining a "tucked hip" position by holding the pelvis in alignment. Athletes may move the arms in conjunction with the legs as in the regular running style. Or, for more advanced balance training, the athletes can perform the drill while reaching upward with the arms, holding the hands behind the head, or while holding a medicine ball. Have athletes do the following:

- Step over—both feet land between each hurdle—lead with the left, lead with the right
- Walkover—only one foot lands between each hurdle
- Backward walkovers and step-overs
- Sideways step over—both feet land between each hurdle, leading with the left and then the right
- Over under (focus on stretching the hip flexors)

WALL KICKS

This drill teaches the athlete to lead with the knee. The athlete begins by standing slightly farther than one leg length away from a sturdy wall. The athlete leans forward from the feet and begins a controlled fall into the wall. The lead leg drives forward (leading with the knee) toward the wall to brace the fall. At the last moment, the lower leg whips forward, and the foot makes contact with the wall at a point higher than the high hurdle settings. Athletes should use the coordinated arm action during this drill, and they should practice using both sides as lead legs.

SINGLE-LEG HURDLING

This drill helps the athlete progress from the very controlled hurdle mobility moves to skills that more closely resemble those used in the competitive event. Begin with five or six hurdles (at the lowest setting) spaced seven foot lengths apart. The athlete begins by walking near the side of the hurdle and practicing the trail leg action in a slow and controlled movement. The athlete repeats the move using the other leg as the trail leg. Next, the athlete walks over the side of the barrier, clearing the hurdle only with the lead leg. The trail leg will pass along the side of the hurdle. As athletes learn the rhythm and technique for the drill, they can begin jogging along the side of the hurdles.

SOFT HURDLES

When athletes are comfortable doing the drills that lead up to hurdling, you can allow them to try the entire move over soft barriers (you may use commercial products such as 3-inch foam risers that can be added to conventional hurdles, or you can simply string athletic tape between two hurdles and use that as the introductory barrier). Begin with one soft barrier and gradually add a second, third, fourth, and so on. After three or four successful practices, athletes can begin clearing the regulation hurdles in workouts.

CHEATED HURDLES

This type of workout involves running over lower barriers or hurdles that are spaced closer together than normal. Cheated hurdling can be used to add hurdling technique work to any type of sprint workout. In other words, acceleration, maximum velocity, and extensive and intensive tempo can be worked on while going over hurdles. The hurdles are moved into positions to allow athletes to rhythmically complete the repetitions without stutter-stepping or reaching for the hurdles. To set up the hurdles, use your feet to measure how far from the marking on the track the hurdles will be positioned. Remember that if the first hurdle is moved in two feet, the second needs to be moved in four feet, the third six feet, and so on. Otherwise, only the first hurdle will be cheated, and the others will be positioned with a regulation distance between barriers.

Relays

Many of your young athletes will likely consider the relays to be their favorite events. These events include a team dynamic that is unique in the sport of track and field. In addition, the relays can be dramatic and exciting. Lead changes, fast handoffs, the risk of mishandling the baton, and the group concept all make relays fun and compelling for athletes, coaches, and fans.

In this section, we introduce techniques for two basic styles of handoff used in the relays. Although the baton exchange is important in every relay, the shorter races demand faster exchanges because the overall race is completed quicker. For this reason, *nonvisual* exchanges are often used for the 4×100-meter relay. For longer relays, the incoming runner often enters the exchange zone under distress, and a safer exchange is preferred. *Visual* exchanges are often used for these longer races.

However, before we discuss the types of exchanges, you should review the following essential considerations that apply for both styles of relay exchange.

- Athletes must identify the marks for each exchange zone. These marks may vary greatly by facility. In some cases, the zones are marked with triangles. On other tracks, the marks might look like a letter T. To be sure about the marks, ask the starter or local coach.

- You should know the rules about uniforms. These rules seem to change frequently and are different depending on the organizing body. Generally, all members of the relay team need to be wearing the same uniform. In some cases, the uniforms need to be exactly the same. Other organizing bodies only require that the color of the uniform be the same but the style could vary. Understand the rules for your circumstance early enough to make proper arrangements.

- The speed of the baton through the exchange zone is critical. Fast runners and slow exchanges will combine to make a mediocre time.

- The incoming runner must approach the zone at a consistent speed. Aggressively bringing the baton into the zone will help the outgoing runner time her takeoff.

- The acceleration of the outgoing runner should be consistent and aggressive.

- The outgoing runner needs to provide a steady hand and a consistent target.

- The incoming runner is responsible for placing the baton in the outgoing runner's hand.

- After receiving the handoff, the runner should not switch the baton to the other hand when competing in a short relay. In longer relays, switching hands is okay but should be practiced.

- Runners should hold the baton near one end so that there is room on the other end for the next runner to grab the baton.

- The coach needs to tactically consider the order of runners on a relay team. For example, the coach should identify which athlete can start well and which athlete would be the best anchor (the anchor needs to be a good competitor). More talented athletes might be better able to handle the stick twice on the second and third leg.

- Runners need to keep the stick moving through the zone. Both runners should be going fast when the baton is exchanged.

Nonvisual Handoff

The most common short relay in which nonvisual handoffs are used is the 4×100-meter relay. Since the track is 400 meters, each athlete runs one-fourth of the oval. Typically, the athlete running the first leg carries the baton in the right hand and passes to the second runner's left hand. The second runner passes to the third runner's right hand, and the anchor runner brings the baton home in the left hand. This right, left, right, left pattern allows the first and third runners, who will be running on the curves, to hug the inside of the lane and pass the baton to the next runner (who will be running a straight) with the baton safely in the middle of the lane. Although this pattern is common practice, it is certainly not mandatory. Coaches may decide to allow children to pass and receive the baton in their dominant hand or use any other combination that is best suited for their group of athletes.

Starts for Nonvisual Exchanges

Nonvisual exchanges are used for shorter events that are run at full speed. In these events, many youth teams will use a block start for the first leg. In a relay, the mechanics and technique used for a block start are the same as in other sprinting events. The one difference is that the athlete must hold the baton. All parts of the athlete's hands must be behind the starting line, but the baton may extend beyond the line.

The baton is held at one end with the pinky, ring, and middle fingers holding the baton against the palm of the hand (see figure 7.9). The thumb and index fingers form a bridge to support the upper body. For athletes who are too small to hold the baton with this grip while in the blocks, an upright starting position is advisable.

Figure 7.9 Proper grip of the baton for relays with block starts.

At the starting command, the first runner accelerates to full speed and races toward the first exchange zone.

Incoming and Outgoing Runners

Incoming runners must work hard to avoid dramatic changes in speed late in their leg. As they approach the zone, they need to stay in their predetermined

Figure 7.10   An outgoing runner's stance when waiting for the incoming runner.

part of the lane (inside for legs 1 and 3, outside for legs 2 and 4) and aggressively attack the zone. In the nonvisual exchange, it is the responsibility of the incoming runner to place the baton in the hand of the outgoing runner.

Outgoing runners position themselves in a stance that will allow acceleration and will allow them to see the incoming runner approach. These positions may vary. Some runners might want to get into a modified three-point stance to simulate the block start. Although this start may be faster, it is not recommended because the athlete will have difficulty seeing the go-mark from such a low position. A fundamentally sound stance would have the athlete slightly crouched with the feet mostly facing forward and the upper body slightly twisted in toward the incoming runner (see figure 7.10). The arms should be set in position to begin the alternate driving arm action characteristic of acceleration mechanics.

As the incoming runner hits the go-mark (see the following section), the outgoing runner turns forward and begins accelerating. At the predetermined point, the outgoing runner moves the receiving hand into position and leaves it there—keeping it as still as possible—until he has received the baton. The outgoing runner must avoid "fishing for the stick" and should keep the hand steady. The incoming runner can see the hand, and it is this runner's job to put the stick in the right place.

Go-Marks

In USATF competition, races that involve a nonvisual exchange allow outgoing runners some space to accelerate before they enter the exchange zone. (This is not permitted in Hershey's program.) The acceleration zone is known as the fly zone or international zone. Athletes are allowed to set a "go-mark" on the track (outside the international zone) to indicate when they should begin running. When the incoming runner hits that mark, it is time to GO!

To make the go-mark, athletes are allowed to use two pieces of athletic tape. The go-mark can be as small as a few inches of tape, or it could be as big as two pieces of tape stretched all the way across the lane. The latter might be good for young children who are just learning the event (although you will go through a lot of tape!). This bigger mark is called a box. It is easier to see when an incoming runner enters the box than when a runner passes a small piece of tape on the track. Establishing the proper position for the go-mark, however, takes a good deal of trial and error. When working on the exchange, both runners must go full speed rather than trying to adjust to make the pass.

If they go full speed and miss the pass, the go-mark can be moved back or forward to adjust, and the runners can try again. If the runners are constantly adjusting speed, establishing a go-mark for full-speed running will be very difficult.

To begin establishing the position for the go-mark, try the following suggestions. If the incoming runner is faster than the outgoing runner, make the mark farther back. If the outgoing runner is faster, make the mark closer. Outgoing runners can start anywhere in between the beginning of the fly zone and the end of the exchange zone. The goal is to start at a place that allows the runner to get close to full speed before receiving the baton. For young children, this usually means starting in the middle of the fly zone, while older children and adolescents often start near the beginning of the fly zone. In other words, the bigger and faster the athlete, the more of the acceleration zone they will use.

From their starting point, the athletes should march back (toe to heel) the number of steps they will use to set the go-mark. Here are some guidelines for the approximate distance from the go-mark to the starting point:

- Small children—8 feet
- Adolescents—12 feet
- Adolescents with a fast incoming runner passing to a slower outgoing runner—up to 25 feet

Exchanges

Three styles of passes are commonly used in nonvisual exchanges: underhand, overhand, and push.

Underhand   The outgoing runner holds the receiving hand in a position very similar to the bridge formed in the starting blocks (see figure 7.11). The hand is held still, slightly behind the hip. The incoming runner uses an upsweep motion to place the baton in the hand.

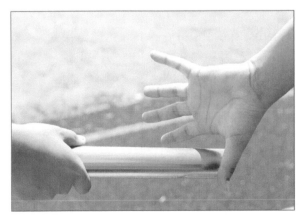

Figure 7.11 Hand position for the underhand exchange.   **Figure 7.12** Hand position for the overhand exchange.

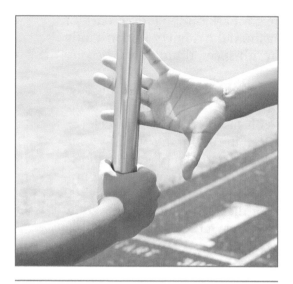

Figure 7.13   Hand position for the push exchange.

Overhand   For an overhand exchange, the outgoing runner holds the receiving hand back with the palm facing up (see figure 7.12). The arm is straight and held higher than the hip. The incoming runner uses a downsweep motion to place the baton in the runner's hand.

Push   For a push exchange, the outgoing runner holds the receiving hand at shoulder height with the thumb down, the palm facing the incoming runner, and the fingers pointing to the inside of the track (see figure 7.13). The incoming runner holds the baton straight up and down and pushes the baton into the hand.

Verbal and Nonverbal Exchanges

Runners who have practiced together for some time begin to get a sense of where the baton will be exchanged in the zone. At this point, the outgoing runner puts the receiving hand in position and the pass is made without a verbal command.

More frequently, however, a command such as "stick" or "hand" is used to indicate when the outgoing runner is to put the hand in position. The incoming runner needs to make the command just before presenting the baton. A common mistake is initiating the passing action and then yelling the command. The outgoing runner then has to process the message and put the receiving hand back. This leaves the incoming runner running for a step or two with the baton extended.

Visual Handoff

Visual, or open, exchanges are used in events that are not as fast. In these events, the incoming runner is often fatigued when entering the exchange zone, and the outgoing runner will have to carefully watch to see when to go. For 8- to 10-year-olds running the 4×100-meter relay, it might be a good idea to start with a visual exchange. As fitness improves, they can begin to work on a nonvisual style. For all athletes running longer relays, the visual exchange is preferred.

Generally, the outgoing runner will wait in position facing the inside of the track. There is no preset "go-mark" as there is in the nonvisual exchange. The outgoing runner must evaluate how fast the incoming runner is approaching and must take off at a time that will allow both runners to be moving. Ideally, the space between the two runners will be equal to the length of both athletes' extended arms. The outgoing runner watches the incoming runner approach, and at the time he deems appropriate, the outgoing runner takes three acceleration steps and puts his hand back to receive the baton. The hand is held at shoulder height, straight out, with the fingers extended to form a big target (see figure 7.14). The incoming runner can bring the baton in with either hand; this runner holds the baton straight up and down and pushes the baton into the hand of the outgoing runner. The outgoing runner usually takes the baton with the left hand. However, if an athlete has a reason not to use the left hand, the athlete may face outside the oval and take the baton with the right hand.

Figure 7.14 The outgoing runner's hand position when receiving the baton for a visual exchange.

Relay Activities

Relay activities are fun for children. You will want to provide a wide range of relay activities from the beginning of the season. Try to include as many members of the training group as possible, and try to think of ways to incorporate relay activities into many different training sessions.

PASSING THE BATON

This is a classic activity that children love to do. A relay team jogs slowly around the outside lanes of the track in a formation based on their running order.

Runners should be about two arm's lengths away from one another. The runner in the back of the pack starts with the baton and passes it to the next runner. When the baton gets to the front of the pack, the front runner places the baton carefully on the track and keeps running. The runner in the back picks up the baton, and the drill is repeated. Proper technique should be emphasized. Both visual and nonvisual exchanges can be practiced in this activity.

VISUAL EXCHANGES WITH RANDOM PARTNERS

The visual exchange is often used when the incoming runner has gone a distance that puts the runner in a state of deep anaerobic fatigue. As a result, incoming runners may have some inconsistency in speed as they approach the exchange zone. Practicing with random partners can help outgoing runners learn how to judge speed and determine when to begin acceleration.

8

Coaching the Distances

I n track and field, the distance runs and race walks are tests of endurance. These events challenge young people to develop strong hearts and lungs, efficient movement patterns, and concentration. The endurance events for youth track and field are scaled down because of developmental considerations, with the longest event typically being two miles or less.

Only a few decades ago, children were known to run from place to place to get where they were going. Unfortunately, today many children spend a great amount of time engaged in the unnatural act of sitting for long periods of time. As a consequence, learning to move economically over distance can seem awkward and uncomfortable for many children. In addition, for many of your young athletes, the training they do at track practice will be their primary running or walking experience. On the other hand, some children may come to youth track with a strong background in other sports that develop endurance. Soccer is the most obvious example. Swimming, basketball, and other team sports can also help children build a level of general fitness that will improve their competitive running or walking on a track.

Children who begin training for endurance events with a base of fitness will obviously have more initial success. Also, it is not uncommon for the best youth athletes to be the best runners. Many others will find their introduction to endurance training to be challenging and potentially frustrating. However, with patience, most children can develop a level of fitness that will support continuous running for two miles. Paying attention to the basic training guidelines described in this chapter can improve efficiency, reduce the chance of injury, and make running more enjoyable.

See table 8.1 for a list of the distance events for each age group for both the USATF Junior Olympics and the Hershey's Track & Field Games.

Table 8.1

USATF Junior Olympics	
Bantam (ages 10 and under)	800-meter run; 1,500-meter run; 1,500-meter race walk
Midget (ages 11 and 12)	800-meter run; 1,500-meter run; 3,000-meter run; 1,500-meter race walk
Youth (ages 13 and 14)	800-meter run; 1,500-meter run; 3,000-meter run; 3,000-meter race walk
Intermediate (ages 15 and 16)	800-meter run; 1,500-meter run; 3,000-meter run; 2,000-meter steeplechase; 5,000-meter race walk
Young (ages 17 and 18)	800-meter run; 1,500-meter run; 3,000-meter run; 2,000-meter steeplechase; 5,000-meter run (young men only); 5,000-meter race walk
Hershey's Track & Field Games	
Ages 9 and 10	No events
Ages 11 and 12	800-meter run
Ages 13 and 14	800-meter run; 1,600-meter run

General Distance-Running Mechanics

Running or walking over distance should be natural. Too often, however, coaches have to patiently teach this movement pattern to sedentary children. To teach fundamentally sound mechanics, you need to have a basic understanding of biomechanics and technique. In this section, we introduce three fundamental mechanical concerns for endurance coaches: heel recovery, stride length, and stride frequency. This will lead into a broader discussion of technique and running style in the section that follows (note that specific information on the mechanics and techniques of race walking is included later in the chapter).

Heel Recovery

The action of the legs in running can be broken into two phases: support and recovery. The pulling and pushing on the track during the support phase is what causes an athlete to move forward. At the completion of the support phase, the leg is behind the body and must be moved in front again to complete the running stroke. As athletes fatigue, it is common to see very low heel recovery. Low heel recovery is inefficient and can cause hamstring injuries. When running, even at a modest pace, young distance runners must work to shorten the recovery leg by bending at the knee and bringing the heel toward the upper hamstring (see figure 8.1a). Some novices shuffle along with their

a   b

Figure 8.1   Heel recovery: (a) correct and (b) incorrect.

feet only coming a few inches off the ground in the recovery phase (see figure 8.1*b*), which actually consumes more energy because the athlete must work harder to bring the long lever of the free leg back into the forward position. This can put enormous force on the hips, hamstrings, and lower back and can increase an athlete's chance for injury. Shortening this lever by bending at the knee as the leg swings forward improves running economy and reduces the chance of injury.

Stride Length and Frequency

When teaching running technique to young athletes, your focus should be on finding the correct stride length for an athlete's strength level and size. Many young children try to run stride for stride with training partners or competitors who are taller or stronger. Although shorter or smaller athletes may run as fast as taller athletes, they need to learn how to do this with quicker steps rather than by overstriding. To develop the proper stride length, an athlete needs to focus on where the foot lands in front of the body, as well as on using effective backside mechanics.

A common misconception is that distance runners should strike the ground heel first. Although this is not necessarily wrong, it is not a general rule for all runners and all types of running. Many people use the heel strike when they are jogging very slowly; for this type of running, the heel strike can be an effective focal point because it helps some people remember to dorsiflex their feet. For running at faster speeds, the foot should land in a flexed position slightly in front of the body, using a backward "pawing" motion and quickly recovering to the front position (the exact distance will vary for each individual and will change as athletes develop). Trying to use a heel strike at speeds faster than a modest jog can result in overstriding. Beyond the stress that overstriding places on the posterior chain, another biomechanical principle at work here is Newton's third law: For every action there is an equal and opposite reaction. Quick, forceful foot contacts propel the runner toward the finish. Slow and long contacts cause the runner to pull the body over the base of support before pushing in the direction of the run. As a coach, you should watch your athletes for signs of overstriding, such as longer ground contact time or bouncing up and down while running. If an athlete complains of shinsplints or pain in the hamstring or lower back, this can also be a sign of overstriding.

The second variable that you can work on with your athletes is efficient backside mechanics. This phase of running encompasses what happens from the time the foot passes under the hips (when the foot is on the ground) until it passes the midline again during the recovery phase. For many novice runners, this phase consumes too much time and can lead to poor posture. Proper technique is to lift the heel forward and upward toward the upper hamstring as soon as it leaves the track. This aggressive lifting helps the hips maintain the tucked position.

Distance-Running Technique

Now that you have a basic understanding of the mechanical principles of running, you can begin to help individual athletes develop a technique or style that is appropriate for them. To do this, you need to focus on three major aspects of technique: posture, arm action, and breathing.

Posture

Competitive running has unique demands. In field sports, players typically adopt a lower hip posture so that they can quickly change directions. On the track, however, it is best to maintain a tall posture to maximize the lever efficiency of the skeleton and the elastic properties of the connective tissue in the hips. Continuous, rhythmic running is also different from the endurance activity in team sports because there are no breaks. Once the starting signal sounds, the race is on until everybody crosses the finish line.

As they get tired, some athletes start to slouch or lose their posture. This tendency needs to be avoided. You should teach athletes that maintaining posture through the end of the race or workout is essential. Slouching when tired actually consumes energy. Every effort should be made to recruit the skeleton to hold up the body. When athletes slouch, their lower back has to work hard to hold up the upper body and the head. For proper posture when running, the head should be kept in a neutral alignment with the spine (see figure 8.2), and the hips should be slightly rolled under the body to keep the spine upright.

You need to make sure that an athlete's attempt to maintain proper posture does not lead to the common mistake of "tightening up." Running stiff like a robot will not be effective; the elasticity of the muscles needs to be allowed to assist in the process. Holding the skeleton in alignment assists in the recruitment of elastic potential. On the other hand, tightness in the chest, arms, and back limits the elasticity and decreases space for the lungs and heart to expand and

Figure 8.2   Proper posture for distance running.

contract. You may find that some athletes are under the assumption that straining in the face and neck will make them go faster. In fact, straining in the face and neck can cause tightness in the body. This is a big problem when tightness constricts the chest. Remember, these events are aerobic—that is, runners need oxygen to create energy to run. When tightness restricts the upper body, it reduces the ability to get oxygen into the lungs.

Arm and Leg Action

When an athlete is distance running, the athlete's arms should move in a coordinated alternate action with the legs. In other words, as the left leg swings forward, the left arm drives back, and as the right leg swings forward, the right arm drives back. This alternate action aids in balance and recruits the muscles of the trunk into the running process. A common mistake related to this is freezing the shoulder joint and accommodating the needed alternate action by shifting the shoulders back and forth. A small amount of motion in the shoulders is acceptable, but too much is a waste of energy.

The positioning of the elbows may vary for distance runners. Some distance runners like to hold their elbows in a fixed position relatively tight to the body. This positioning is okay as long as there is rotation at the shoulder joint. Some runners leave their elbows relatively open. This will work too as long as it does not cause the shoulders to freeze up or cause tightness in the rest of the upper body. The most common style is for runners to modestly open and close the elbow joint in alternate coordination with the legs. When the left leg opens up and moves back to contact the running surface, the right arm swings back and opens a bit at the elbow. As the leg moves forward, the opposite arm shortens by bending at the elbow and swings forward from the shoulder.

Breathing

Young athletes often experience side aches as they begin training for long-distance running. A side ache is a muscle cramp in the diaphragm. As demand for oxygen increases during prolonged activity, the diaphragm pushes downward to create room for the lower part of the lungs to expand. Many young athletes pull their belly in during inhalation, which pushes the diaphragm up. During moderate activity, this is not usually a problem. However, during exertion, the habit of upper chest breathing will cause the thin diaphragm muscle to quickly fatigue and ultimately cramp when in conflict with the need for the lungs to expand. The solution is to teach belly breathing, or pushing the belly out during inhalation. If side aches are not a problem, spending time on belly breathing technique may not be necessary. For children who experience the discomfort of side aches, working on the belly breathing technique during warm-ups and workouts is a worthwhile investment in time.

Training for Distance Running

Training should prepare athletes physiologically by offering progressively more challenging stimuli to train the energy systems, heart, lungs, and muscles. Training should also prepare athletes tactically so that they have an understanding of what will happen with their body during competition.

Children should begin with a general training program. Specificity can increase with age. Training needs to be designed to meet the interests and goals of the members of the training group. In many cases, the coach can provide for specific needs of individuals while orchestrating a workout where everyone is doing the same thing, only at different paces. The workouts and training activities described in the upcoming section provide some ideas on how to meet the developmental needs of athletes within the framework of a group workout. When developing an endurance training regimen for your athletes, you first need to consider these four concepts:

1. *Consistency.* Distance runners need to make running a habit. Children who are new to running should quickly advance to doing some form of endurance running up to three or four days per week. Advanced adolescents can run five or six days per week.

2. *Variability and training the whole athlete.* Although consistency is important, children should not do the same run every day because they will quickly get bored and lose interest in running. Training for the distance events can be fun and interesting with the use of alternative activities that are developmentally appropriate, such as general strength circuits and activities that promote general athleticism.

3. *Progressive loading.* When designing the training schedule, begin very conservatively and progress cautiously. Keep good records and chart the increase in training load. The training load is affected by both volume and intensity. As the championships approach toward the end of the season, the overall volume is dropped and intensity is raised.

4. *Rest, recovery, and regeneration.* Once an athlete is involved in an interesting training program and tastes success in competition, it is easy for the athlete to slip into a cycle of overtraining. Indeed, all athletes need to invest as much thought and energy into recovery and regeneration as they do into their workouts. Variables that athletes (with the help of their parents) can control include making sure the athlete gets enough sleep, eats well, and has a positive attitude. Coaches should provide periodic recovery weeks (e.g., three weeks of progressively harder training followed by a recovery week). Also, coaches can encourage rest and recovery by allowing breaks from training for family vacations and holidays.

Distance-Running Activities

The activities presented here provide work on the different elements of training needed by all distance runners. The activities are divided into three categories: ancillary training, fartlek training, and pace and speed work.

Ancillary Training

Ancillary training refers to activities that support the goal of effective running but are not specific to distance running. These activities help distance runners (and walkers) build the foundation they need to be successful. Ancillary training works to develop the whole athlete. Stronger, well-rounded athletes are less prone to injury and will be able to tolerate more strenuous specific training later in the developmental cycle.

PUSH-UPS

Athletes assume a traditional push-up position with weight distributed evenly over both hands and with either the toes or the knees on the ground. The muscles in the trunk are flexed, and the back is kept straight with the head in alignment with the spine. To perform push-ups, the athlete bends the elbows to lower the body down to the ground and then raises it back up again.

SIT-UPS

Athletes assume a traditional sit-up position with the knees bent and the feet flat on the ground. The muscles of the trunk are flexed, and the back is kept straight with the head in alignment with the spine. To perform sit-ups, the athlete lowers the back down to the ground and then raises it back up again. You can mix up the program and let athletes choose the specific style to be used that day, such as "V style" sit-ups, partner sit-ups, or oblique crunches.

BODY WEIGHT SQUATS

Athletes stand with the feet flat on the ground and shoulder-width apart. The muscles of the trunk are flexed, and the back is kept straight with the hands held down at the sides. While keeping their weight on the heels, athletes bend the knees to lower the body down and then straighten the knees to rise back up.

LUNGES

While standing, athletes step out with one leg, bending it at the knee so that the lower part of the front leg is straight up and down and in line with the knee. The athletes push back off the front leg to the standing position and repeat the move with the other leg.

Fartlek Training

Fartlek training is commonly used by distance runners. The word *fartlek* is Swedish and means "speed play." The basic idea of this training is to run at various intensities during the course of one workout. Bursts of high-intensity running are alternated with periods of an easier, or recovery, pace. Although this type of training can be done randomly early in the season or during a recovery week, coaches usually use more structured fartlek training so they can carefully monitor and record training loads. Structured fartlek training can be done using time or distance to measure the high-intensity bursts.

LEAP FROG

Athletes form a single-file line and begin running at a comfortable pace about two to five meters apart from one another. The runner in the back of the line surges forward, passes everyone, and assumes the position as the leader. After a short period of running at an easy pace, the runner who is now at the end of the pack surges forward and assumes the lead. The process continues for the period prescribed by the coach, or the coach can set the length of the activity based on the number of surges. For example, if there are 10 runners in the group and each runner surges twice—with a 30-second period of easy running in between each surge—that would create a 12- to 15-minute fartlek with 20 surges (50-meter surges).

ULTIMATE FRISBEE

This fun activity can be used early in the season or during a recovery week to provide athletes with some easy running and plenty of fast surges. The game is easy to learn even for young children, and the only needed skill is the ability to catch and throw a Frisbee. The game is similar to soccer except that once an athlete catches the Frisbee, the athlete must come to a stop and throw to a teammate. A score happens when someone catches the Frisbee in the end zone of a football field or beyond the end line of a soccer field.

Pace

Running at a smooth and consistent pace improves economy and overall success. The following activities will help you teach pace to your athletes.

FOLLOW THE RABBIT

Athletes run in a pack led by a runner who has a solid sense of pace. For workouts at a youth track practice, the rabbit could be an older runner or a member of the group who has already developed pacing ability. The coach shouts split times at determined points so that the developing runners learn what certain paces feel like.

REPEATS

This type of pace training focuses on running efforts of higher quality and intensity. As such, the recovery time between repeats is quite long. Typically, repeats are done at intensive tempo. Distances can vary from 75-meter repeats for the beginning runners to 600-meter repeats for advanced athletes. Volume ranges will vary considerably depending on experience and ability. The key is to determine a volume that allows the athlete to finish the workout while maintaining high quality throughout. The workout should be challenging, but if the athlete is dramatically slowing or is otherwise unable to maintain a steady pace, the intensity should be reduced.

INTERVALS

This type of workout focuses on quantity and developing the capacity to run at a steady pace while fatigued. During interval training, the rest period is minimal and the next running effort begins before the athlete is fully recovered. Intervals can be done at both intensive and extensive tempos. Again, the coach should shout split times at designated points to help the runners learn what certain paces feel like as they get tired.

Race Walking

Race walking is a part of the Junior Olympics program, and this event provides more athletes with a chance to compete in endurance events. Children with good aerobic potential who learn proper race-walking technique can sometimes find high levels of success in these events. Race walkers who are competitive at the highest international levels are outstanding aerobic athletes who would likely be successful in other disciplines. However, because of the minimal number of athletes competing at the grassroots level in the United States, average long-distance runners with a passion for training and a willingness to learn might find an opportunity to advance far in race walking—even to championship events.

Although the opportunities for youth are mostly limited to USA Track & Field's Junior Olympics program, there are some opportunities for college-aged athletes to compete in race walking, including in the NAIA. A number of NAIA colleges and universities give scholarships to race walkers, but there are few candidates because high schools do not offer the event. Promoting race walking at the club level can help build the pool for college recruiters. Also, race walking is part of the program in high-level international competition. But without having the event as part of the high school program in this country, we have a very small pool of athletes to choose from when selecting the U.S. national team. Consequently, American performance in these events on the international level is rarely in the top tier. Exposing children to the race walks is good for the overall health of the sport. Coaches interested in becoming more knowledgeable about teaching and training race walkers can find support on the USATF Web site.

Race-Walking Technique

Walking differs from running in that there is no flight phase. Running, even at a slow pace, involves a push-off of the back leg and some flight before landing on the front leg. The rules for race walking mandate that the athlete must stay in constant contact with the surface. In other words, the front foot must make contact before the back foot comes off the ground. Failure to maintain contact is a violation called *lifting*. The other important rule for race-walking competition is that the front leg must land straight and stay locked out until the hips pass over the foot. No bend is allowed in the knee until the leg is perpendicular to the ground.

The key to walking fast is to maximize the potential of the hips. Good walkers demonstrate large oscillations in the hips and a very deliberate forward push. This signature technique is what some people find a bit curious the first time they observe it at a track meet. Since there is no push off the ground (or flight phase) in walking, this aggressive hip action is used to increase stride length. Stride length is limited by how much extension the walker can get from reaching with the hips. Therefore, to go faster, stride frequency must be improved.

The arms are typically held close to the body with a fairly tight bend at the elbow. As in running, the arms move opposite the legs and aid in force production and balance. One arm is aggressively driven backward as the opposite leg moves backward under the hips.

In addition, as with all events in track and field, maintaining posture is critical in race walking. Proper posture is demonstrated by staying tall, keeping the upper body loose but upright, and keeping the head in a neutral alignment with the spine. As with sprinting and long-distance running, weakness in the hips and trunk can lead to bending over slightly (or tipping the hips forward) during fatigue. This is always a warning sign that the risk of injury is significantly increased.

Race-Walking Activities

The walks are definitely a specialty, and dedicated training is a prerequisite for success. However, a general approach to endurance training is appropriate for most beginners. How much training is dedicated to walking and how much to other aerobic work (such as running, swimming, or cycling) is an individual concern. Some children might compete in both walks and runs at meets. Others may want to focus exclusively on the walks. In any case, put some high-intensity walking workouts into the program before competition so that the athlete is prepared for the unique demands of the event.

HIP MOBILITY EXERCISES WITH HURDLES

Obviously, there are no barriers to jump over in a race-walking competition; however, you can use hurdles to help athletes increase the range of motion and strength of their hips. Set six hurdles at a height that will allow smaller athletes to stand astride the hurdle. Athletes walk forward, sideways, and backward over the hurdles. The athletes should concentrate on using a large range of motion in the hips and maintaining good posture. They should bring the heel close to the upper hamstring and move the knee out and up when clearing the hurdle.

IT BAND FLEXIBILITY

To walk quickly, great range of motion is needed in the hips. The iliotibial band (or IT band) runs down the side of the upper leg and inserts near the knee. If this connective tissue is overstressed, significant pain can develop in the knee, and walking can become very uncomfortable. To help prevent injury, your athletes need to develop IT band flexibility. The following exercises can be used to improve this flexibility (these exercises should be used as part of the warm-up and cool-down on workout days and as a main part of a recovery workout):

- *Pigeon.* This move derives from yoga. Athletes begin in a kneeling position and move one leg straight back. They move the other leg into a position similar to sitting with crossed legs. The spine should be kept perpendicular to the ground.
- *Side plank hip lifts.* Athletes form a plank by posting on one elbow and the sides of the feet. This plank position could be described as a sideways pushup, but instead of lifting the body with the one arm posted on the ground, the hips alternately dip and lift. This motion is like a side bend from a plank position.
- *Knee hug crosses.* Athletes begin by sitting on the track with the legs straight out in front. The athlete bends one leg, bringing the leg up and placing the foot near the outside of the straight leg. The athlete bends the torso forward and twists toward the bent leg using the arms to draw the body and upper leg together.
- *Physio ball work.* Exercises using physio (or Swiss) balls provide a dynamic challenge to the stabilizer muscles. Lying on the ball in various positions provides a stretch for the side of the body.

FORM WALKING

To train for race walking, an athlete needs to spend a significant amount of time doing lower-intensity walking with good race-walking form, somewhat similar to how athletes use jogging to train for running. However, different from jogging, this lower-intensity walking should include a concentrated effort to maintain the technique that will be used in competition. This type of walking helps the athlete develop all aspects of style as well as the specific strength needed for postural endurance. This walking is part of the warm-up routine for hard workouts and competition. Because it is performed at lower intensity, the volume of this type of walking can be higher. Submaximal bouts of walking should feel comfortable for athletes for at least 5 to 10 minutes beyond the length of time it takes to complete the race distance in competition.

9

Coaching the Jumps

Jumping events are contested for height or distance. The jumps contested for height are called the *vertical jumps*, which include the high jump and the pole vault. The jumps contested for distance are known as the *horizontal jumps*, which include the running long jump, the standing long jump, and the triple jump. See table 9.1 for a list of the jumping events for each age group for both the USATF Junior Olympics and the Hershey's Track & Field Games.

Table 9.1

USATF Junior Olympics	
Bantam (ages 10 and under)	High jump, long jump
Midget (ages 11 and 12)	High jump, long jump
Youth (ages 13 and 14)	High jump, pole vault, long jump, triple jump
Intermediate (ages 15 and 16)	High jump, pole vault, long jump, triple jump
Young (ages 17 and 18)	High jump, pole vault, long jump, triple jump
Hershey's Track & Field Games	
Ages 9 and 10	Standing long jump
Ages 11 and 12	Standing long jump
Ages 13 and 14	Standing long jump

Standing Long Jump

The standing long jump is an event in the Hershey program. In this event, the athlete lines up with the feet fixed on a line, crouches down, and leaps out as far as possible into a landing area (see figure 9.1 for an example of the standing long jump area). Although this seems simple enough, young athletes who participate in the standing long jump should develop their skill level in practice before competing. Practice will help strengthen the body, reduce the chance of injury, and develop the specific attributes of technique and explosiveness that contribute to jumping farther. Additionally, the standing long jump can be used as an excellent training tool for your athletes—sprinters

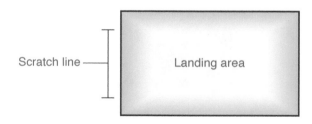

Figure 9.1   Standing long jump area.

and throwers included—to test hip and leg power. As a coach, plan to have your athletes test several times a season using the standing long jump to chart their improvement.

Standing Long Jump Technique

When an athlete is preparing to execute the standing long jump, the athlete's feet must be fixed in a parallel position. The jumper may rock the toes and heels off the surface, but the feet cannot be lifted completely off the surface before the jump. The athlete rocks the arms back and forth and bends at the knees and hips to set up the appropriate rhythm and body position for a good jump.

> **Coaching Tip**
> Young athletes often try to take a "gather step" when attempting to jump for height or distance. Although this extra step will increase the result for most children, it is against the rules for track and field. Teach athletes that they should concentrate on developing a strong and stable base when jumping to help break this habit.

To begin the jump, the athlete swings both arms forcefully forward in unison, as shown in figure 9.2a, and blocks—or stops—them slightly higher than the shoulders, with a slight yet firm bend at the elbow. Both feet must leave the ground at the same time so that a full extension of the ankles, knees, and hips—also called *triple extension*—must be achieved in order to use all potential energy from these joints (see figure 9.2b).

Just as the athlete is about to land, the feet should be as far in front of the body as possible without causing the athlete to lose balance and take a backward step after landing. To get the feet to move forward, the arms whip back to the hips. This helps kick the feet out in front. On landing, the athlete should try to absorb the impact by bending at the knees and hips (see figure 9.2c).

a   b   c

Figure 9.2 Standing long jump.

Standing Long Jump Activities

Standing long jump activities are a fun way to harness your athletes' interest in the event and to increase their skill level and success. Remember, too, that the standing long jump is a great training tool for sprinters and throwers as well. For these activities, you should reinforce the following aspects of technique: fixed feet, triple extension, and absorbing the landing. For most children, 2 sets of 5 repetitions would be an appropriate amount for each jumping activity. Advanced jumpers could do 3 sets of 10 repetitions.

FROG JUMP

Athletes begin by standing on both feet and rocking down by bending at the hips and knees until the hands just touch the ground. At this point, they explode up and out of the crouched position by extending the knees and hips and driving the arms up. The landing is a rhythmical transition into another repetition of rocking down into position and then jumping. For variation, these jumps can be done on one leg or on a slight incline. Landing at a higher level than the takeoff decreases the impact and allows the ankle joint to stretch, thus working the ankle over a greater range of motion.

PARTNER SHOULDER HOLDS

Pair your athletes up with a partner who is similar in size and strength. One athlete stands behind the other with both hands on the partner's shoulders. The athlete in front attempts to jump while the partner presses down on the athlete's shoulders. Enough resistance should be provided to challenge the jumping athletes while allowing continued upward motion. Performing 1 to 3 sets of 10 jumps once or twice a week will provide resistance training specific to jumping.

ROCKET JUMP

Athletes load into position by bending at the knees and waist so that they are in a crouched position with the arms held back. This position is similar to the starting position for the standing long jump. The feet are parallel and face forward, the back is straight, and the head is aligned with the spine. However, for rocket jumps, the goal is to jump straight up, not out. To execute the jump, the athlete extends the knees, hips, and ankles; shoots the arms straight up into the air; and reaches high into the air with the arms. The athlete lands on both feet. As in the competitive standing long jump, athletes should absorb the landing by bending at the ankles, knees, and hips. For variation, this jump can be done on one leg, or the landing can be on one or two feet. This jump can also be performed using a rotation (left or right) where the athlete adds a bit of a twist into the loading phase of the jump and rotates 180 or 360 degrees while in the air.

TUCK JUMP

The tuck jump is very similar to the rocket jump. The initial stance, jumping sequence, and landing are the same for both jumps. The difference in the tuck jump is that while in the air, the athlete quickly brings both knees toward the chest, and the arms are swung down to the hips to help bring the legs forward. Again, this move can be made more challenging by jumping off one leg. For a one-leg tuck jump, the jumping leg is brought up to the chest, and the opposite leg is left down for balance.

SPEEDSKATER JUMP

For this move, the goal is not to go up, but rather from side to side. This helps develop the lateral stabilizers of the legs and hips. The preliminary position is similar to that for the previous jumps. Rather than jumping up, however, athletes jump off the outside foot toward their side. As athletes land and absorb the impact, they are also loading the other leg for the next jump. Athletes continue jumping back and forth with rhythm until the desired number of repetitions is reached.

SNOWBOARDER JUMP

Again, for this move the starting position and the landing are the same as in the previous jumps. But in the snowboarder jump, athletes arch back while in the air and try to touch their feet with one hand. Many children will be familiar with the move because it is a common trick for snowboarders.

Long Jump

The long jump is contested at a venue consisting of a long runway, a takeoff board, and a sand pit (see figure 9.3). This event tests speed and jumping ability. Many of your athletes will likely be very eager to participate in the long jump. Sprinting down the runway, leaping off of one foot, sailing through the air, and finally, splashing into the sand pit is great fun for many children.

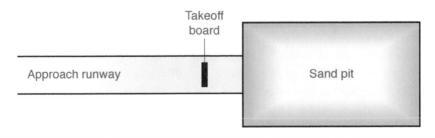

Figure 9.3   Long jump area.

General Mechanics for Jumps With an Approach

Let's consider a few mechanical elements of the jumps that require an approach run—the long jump, high jump, pole vault, and triple jump (the standing long jump as discussed previously does not require an approach run). These principles are fundamental to jumping events at all developmental levels.

Approach Run

For jumps with an approach, the run must be made at an appropriate speed. This is called the *maximum controllable speed*. It is as close to maximum speed as the athlete can get while still being able to hit the correct takeoff position. The coach and athlete work together to determine how close to full-speed running the athlete can get and still execute a consistent and effective takeoff. Inconsistent approaches cause fouls in the long jump and triple jump. In the vertical jumps (high jump and pole vault), consistent approaches are necessary to hit the correct takeoff position. Athletes need to develop the ability to be consistent during practice. Those athletes who have developed a consistent and effective approach run in practice will be much more confident and effective in competition. Struggling to hit the correct takeoff position in meets is frustrating.

Penultimate Step

For jumps with an approach, the next-to-last step—called the *penultimate step*—is extremely important. This step sets up the body for an effective takeoff. On the penultimate step, the athlete uses a slight lowering of the hips to prepare for a transfer of horizontal momentum into a vertical lift. To lower the hips, the athlete bends at the knee of the support leg while keeping the spine perpendicular to the ground. Bending at the hips during the penultimate step is an indication of poor posture. The more vertical lift needed for the jump, such as in the high jump, the more noticeable the penultimate step will be.

Posture

For jumps with an approach, solid posture must be maintained in order for the forces of the jumping action to result in a good distance. To maintain solid posture, athletes should run tall and upright down the runway while holding their hips under their body and keeping their head neutral with the spine. Young athletes may believe they can add to the force of the jump by whipping their head to the side or back and getting really low at takeoff; in fact, this action disrupts the effective movement. Another common problem for young athletes is a weakness in the hips that may absorb the ground reaction forces and reduce the overall result. Ground reaction forces could be described as "bounce." Running with poor posture is like trying to bounce a flat ball—the loose covering absorbs the bounce just as weak hips absorb the bounce of the runner. Running with good posture maximizes ground reaction. As a coach, you can increase your athletes' awareness of their posture by using coaching cues such as "run tall" and by helping athletes develop core stability through trunk-strengthening exercises.

Long Jump Technique

In this section, we begin with some initial concerns regarding long jump technique and then discuss the different phases of the long jump: approach run, takeoff, flight, and landing.

When teaching your athletes the mechanics of the long jump, you first need to address the following two concerns:

1. *Determining the correct foot for the jump*

   Most athletes will prefer to jump off their strong-side leg, using the quick-side leg for an aggressive forward and upward swinging action (as discussed later on page 121). Here are a few simple tests you can use to help athletes determine their strong side and their quick side:

   - Stand behind the athlete and gently push him to see which leg goes out for support. Generally the athlete will step out to support with the quick leg.

   - Place a soccer ball on the grass, and have the athlete take a three- to five-meter run at it and kick it as far as possible. Generally, the strong leg will brace, and the quick leg will do the kicking.

   - Watch athletes play recreational basketball, and observe if they more consistently execute layups off of one leg or the other. Typically, they will jump off of the strong leg and drive the knee of the quick leg up.

   You need to determine an athlete's strong side and quick side; however, you should remember that the athlete's long-term development will benefit if the athlete learns how to jump off of both feet and practices doing so as much as possible. This is called *bilateral training* and will help reduce the chance of athletes hitting performance plateaus early in their sport career. Of course, the coach and athlete should determine which foot is most effective for competition and should make sure that practice prepares the athlete for the meets.

2. *Determining the length of the approach*

   In youth track, long jumpers often make the mistake of using the entire length of the runway for their approach. Children can use a shorter approach because it takes less time and energy to accelerate a little person's body up to full speed. In fact, short approaches of six to eight takeoff steps (approximately 50 to 80 feet) enable children to build up enough speed for an effective jump. The runway itself could be as long as 150 feet (many youth programs use high school or college venues). When children begin at the end of the runway, they are often tired and slowing down by the time they make the jump.

   For a general idea of where an athlete should start on the runway, you can use what is called a *run-back*. For the run-back, the athlete starts at the takeoff board in the appropriate initial stance, with the heel of the jumping foot at the scratch line (see figure 9.3 on page 117 for an example of the long jump competition area). Using a correct approach technique (as discussed in the following section), the athlete counts out six to eight takeoff steps. In counting takeoff steps, the athlete only counts the foot that will be used for jumping, or every other foot contact. At the end of the run-back, the jumper finishes with a pop-up. For more advanced youth athletes, there will be about 10 feet between takeoff steps; however, smaller children obviously have smaller strides. The coach or a training partner stands beside the runway to watch for where the athlete's jumping foot lands at the end of the run-back. A marker is placed on the side of the runway, and this becomes the starting mark. Some adjustment will have to be made as athletes get more warmed up or start fatiguing.

Long Jump Approach

Now that the jumping leg and approach length are determined, the athlete may begin practicing the run-up. The approach run can be broken down into three phases: starting position and acceleration, middle of the run, and transition into the jump.

Starting Position and Acceleration   At track meets, you will see many children using the starting position for the jumps as a chance to show their unique

style, but the key is to develop an approach that is consistent and accurate. The crouch start is a simple style that puts athletes in a good position to accelerate. In the crouch start, the toe of the jumping foot is positioned in the middle of the runway—lined up with the athlete's mark—and the opposite leg is placed back about two feet (see figure 9.4). The arms are held in a running position on alternate sides from the legs (left foot forward, left arm back). The athlete crouches down into a comfortable and balanced position and begins the acceleration with an aggressive step, pushing off the front leg and strongly driving the arms. The first few steps are aggressive and complete pushes down the runway.

Figure 9.4   Initial starting position for the long jump approach run.

Middle of the Run   As athletes accelerate down the runway, they should be near top speed by the middle of the run. Late acceleration can strain the hamstrings and make it difficult to be consistent at the end of the run. The middle of the run is characterized by tall posture and balanced, smooth strides.

Transition Into the Jump   As the athlete approaches the board at the end of the runway, a subtle quickening of the stride frequency occurs as the athlete prepares to jump. At this point of the run, the athlete should be at maximum controllable speed.

Long Jump Takeoff

Assuming the athlete is jumping off the left foot, the step with the right foot immediately before the board will be the penultimate step (see figure 9.5*a*). This next-to-last foot contact is when the takeoff begins. Naturally, athletes will "settle" slightly to prepare to transfer their horizontal momentum to a vertical lift. This is demonstrated by a subtle lowering of the hips. The spine remains erect, and the head should stay in alignment. Every effort should be made to preserve runway speed. Lowering the hips too much causes the athlete to slow down and should be avoided. From the settled position, the back leg swings aggressively up and forward as the jumping foot hits the takeoff board (see figure 9.5*b*). The takeoff foot should land flat on the board for more traction, stability, and power. Additionally, the arm action at takeoff is similar to an exaggerated running stroke. Again, for left-footed jumpers, the left arm will swing aggressively forward with the right leg. The right arm will rip back at the point of takeoff.

a   b

Figure 9.5   Body positioning for the long jump takeoff.

Figure 9.6   Body positioning for the long jump flight.

Long Jump Flight

As mentioned previously, the takeoff position looks like an exaggerated running stroke. From this position, the front arm reaches up, and the back arm completes its rotation until both arms are above the head. At this point, the athlete will "hang" and make the body as long as possible as he sails through the air. The legs hang low to increase the length of the body during flight. Making the body as long as possible helps to slow down the naturally occurring forward rotation (see figure 9.6).

Long Jump Landing

As the athlete begins to descend, the arms are whipped down to the sides of the body past the hips. This causes the feet to kick out, which will increase the distance of the jump and make for a safer landing. On impact, the athlete should try to absorb the forces by bending at the knees and hips.

Long Jump Activities

Training for the long jump includes practicing the run-up, jumping technique, the flight phase, and landing. Training should also be designed to develop the physical attributes that contribute to farther jumps: speed, jumping ability, and postural strength. Improving technique and physical attributes will lead to longer jumps and more success in the event.

RUNWAY REHEARSAL

Use chalk or tape to set up a temporary "runway" on the track. Athletes can practice finding their mark and making slight adjustments based on coaches' observations. Athletes should have the opportunity to perform 6 to 10 runway rehearsals on the track per week.

POP-UPS

This activity can be used to teach your athletes how to achieve lift and stay vertical. Pop-ups are essentially the long jump action without the regular type of landing. At the landing, the athlete uses running action and absorbs the landing by taking a few steps. Athletes should begin with short approaches so that the focus is on the vertical lift; they can progress to popping up after a full runway approach. Mastering the pop-up with a full approach is important for more advanced athletes because the subtle lowering of the hips at the penultimate step changes the stride length.

OBJECT JUMPS

Jumping over safe and appropriate objects is a beginner activity that can help young athletes learn how to jump off of one foot and convert their horizontal momentum into vertical lift. Objects can be placed at the beginning of the sand pit. Children take a short approach down the runway and attempt to clear the object and then land on their feet in the sand. Think carefully about the objects you choose. Commercial products such as foam hurdles are available. Or, you could use something as simple as a pizza box propped up like a tent. Never use real hurdles, benches, or something that might cause athletes to trip or would hurt athletes if they land on it.

RAMP JUMP

While ramp jumps are not exactly specific to the competitive event, they can be great for practicing the mechanics of flight and landing because they allow athletes to jump farther with less effort. A ramp can be quickly fashioned, for example, by placing a 4-by-8-foot sheet of plywood (1 inch thick) on two car tires lying flat on the runway. You could also use commercial springboards for this activity—the type of springboards that are often used for gymnastics. Begin by having athletes use a short approach (20 feet) so they can get used to jumping off the ramp. Gradually move the starting point back as athletes become consistent with the short approach. Athletes should perform approximately 20 jumps, once a week.

Triple Jump

The triple jump is contested in an area that is very similar to the long jump venue, with the main difference being that there are multiple takeoff boards set back several feet from the sand. While in the long jump there is usually only one board that all competitors use, the triple jump includes two, three, or four takeoff boards for the athlete to choose from (see figure 9.8). Beginners might choose to use the board closest to the sand, while advanced jumpers might choose to use the board farthest from the pit. Once competition has started, athletes are not permitted to change boards.

The technique consists of a linear approach run followed by a hop, step, and jump into the sand. The hop is initiated at the selected board. The next two foot contacts happen on the runway surface; however, the overall distance from the takeoff board is measured for the result of the jump. This event is part of the USATF Junior Olympics program, but only some states offer the triple jump.

Figure 9.8 Triple jump area.

Triple Jump Technique

This section is divided into three parts based on the different aspects of technique for the triple jump. First, the approach run is discussed. Next, the jump itself—that is, the hop, step, and jump—is introduced. And finally, information about the flight and landing is provided.

Triple Jump Approach Run

The approach run for the triple jump is very similar to the approach run for the long jump where the speed and rhythm of the run are crucial. However, most children will need slightly less speed in the triple jump than in the long jump. The coach and athlete should work together to find an approach tempo that will allow the athlete to be successful in the phases of the jump. Too fast and the athlete might not have control during those phases. Too slow and the athlete will not reach her potential.

Hop, Step, and Jump for the Triple Jump

When the athlete reaches the takeoff board, the athlete begins a series of three controlled horizontal jumps before landing in the sand pit. These jumps are called *phases of the triple jump*—the first is a hop, the second is a step, and the third is a jump—as discussed in the following sections.

Before we go into the specific phases, you should note a few key points related to all three phases of the triple jump:

- For each phase of the triple jump, a good, tall posture is especially important. Maintaining erect posture allows the skeletal system to support some of the jarring from the impacts,and takes some of the force off of the connective tissue. Stability starts with good posture of the foot. The foot should be dorsiflexed (the foot is flexed upward toward the knee, with the ankle at 90 degrees). If the feet are dangling during the phases of the triple jump, this can result in various injuries.

- A double arm action can be used for each of the three phases. For the initial takeoff from the board, the double arm action is set up by putting both arms back behind the hips during the next-to-last foot contact. At takeoff, both arms are driving forward and up aggressively. For the next two phases, the arms rotate behind the hips while the athlete is in the air, and the forward and upward drive is repeated with each foot contact. The key is to actively use the arms to help balance and to generate more force into the jumps during the phases.

- The distance covered in each of these phases should be about equal. For example, in a 30-foot jump, the athlete should cover about 10 feet in each of the phases. The sound of the foot contacts through the phases should have a consistent tempo.

Hop   In the first phase, the hop, the athlete must land on the same foot that hit the takeoff board (see figure 9.9, *a-c*). Many athletes jump off the board

Figure 9.9   Hop phase for the "hop, step, and jump" for the triple jump.

in the triple jump using the opposite foot they use in the long jump. The hop phase is challenging because jumpers have to "cycle through" and get the foot they took off from back into position to land and then jump from it again. Because of this, many children feel comfortable using their quick foot for the hop. Using the quick foot (in most cases, the opposite foot used for the long jump) helps change the pattern of a long jump takeoff to a lower, more controlled, triple jump takeoff. In addition, using the quick foot first puts the strong leg in the final position to jump into the sand. The final phase is most similar to the long jump, and it is good to have the strong foot in position for the leap into the sand.

Step   In the second phase, the step, the athlete leaps from the landing position of the first phase onto the opposite foot (see figure 9.10). Moving off of one foot and onto the other foot is the definition of a "step." However, unlike a walking or running step, the goal is to cover a great distance. A common mistake is to have a big hop, a small step, and a big final jump. Again, it is more efficient to keep the phases about the same distance. The best way to accomplish this is to have a relatively conservative hop and a very aggressive step.

Jump   In the third phase, the jump, the athlete lands from the step, makes the final jump into the sand pit, and lands similar to when executing the long jump (see figure 9.11). The jump needs to be very aggressive because much of the speed from the runway will be lost in the landings of the first two phases. The athlete will need to be very explosive to generate distance on the jump into the sand.

Figure 9.10   Step phase for the "hop, step, and jump" for the triple jump.

Figure 9.11   Jump phase for the "hop, step, and jump" for the triple jump.

Triple Jump Flight and Landing

The flight and landing for the triple jump are similar to the flight and landing for the long jump. The athlete leaves the arms above the head after the final double arm drive and reaches up into the air (as previously shown in figure 9.6). The legs hang low to keep the body long. As the athlete approaches the sand, both arms are whipped down to the sides, causing the legs to come up (see figure 9.12). On impact, the athlete absorbs the landing by bending at the hips and knees.

Figure 9.12   Body positioning for the triple jump landing.

Triple Jump Activities

Like the event itself, training for the triple jump is very demanding. Be patient when introducing young athletes to the event. It is better to train too little and come back the next day than it is to do too much and risk an overuse injury.

BOUNDING

Bounding involves performing aggressive rhythmic jumps on a flat surface. This activity can be used to work on all aspects of technique: equal-distance phases, arm action, posture, rhythm, cycling through, stability, and so on. For beginners, set cones 10 meters apart to designate the start and end lines, advancing to 20 to 25 meters apart as athletes increase their skill level. Bounding moves that your athletes can use include the following:

- Repetitive hops on one leg (i.e., LLL, and so on; then RRR, and so on)
- Speed hops (i.e., set these up as races or use a timer)
- Repetitive triple jump sequence (i.e., LLRLLRLLR and then RRLRRLRRL, and so on)
- Alternating legs (i.e., RLRLRL, and so on)
- Skips for height or distance

GRADUATED PHASE JUMPS

This drill helps teach the rhythm of jumping with equal distance through the phases of the triple jump. A grid is set up on a grassy area beside the sand pit. Three diagonal lines are painted on the grass to indicate where the athletes' feet should land. The lines start about 1 meter apart and remain equidistant from each other as they spread out to a width of 4 to 5 meters. The coach uses the lines on the grid to teach athletes how far to go on each phase to maintain an even spacing. To begin, the athlete takes a very short approach run (less than 20 feet) to build up a little speed before the hop. The narrow part of the grid should be set so that novices can make the pit from a standing start (less than 2 meters or about 4 to 5 feet between lines on the grid). The wide end of the grid is set so that your advanced athletes can make the pit from a short approach (as much as 15-foot spacing for advanced adolescents, although more likely about 12 feet for most). If your athletes master the drill at the farthest distance, they can focus on consistency and quality. There is no need for athletes to attempt jumping for maximum distance in this drill. Jumping for distance should be done when using a traditional runway approach.

DOUBLE JUMP

This drill removes the hop phase and allows athletes to concentrate on the last two-thirds of the triple jump. It is an advanced drill that should only be used with children who have mastered the basic hop, step, and jump sequence. For this drill, a temporary takeoff position is marked (using cones, tape, or chalk), and the athlete uses a very short approach (three or four takeoff steps, six to eight total foot contacts). Once athletes get the hang of the drill, they will be able to go about 50 to 60 percent of their competitive distance for the full triple jump. So, make the takeoff spot about that distance from the place that they normally land in the sand. After getting the takeoff position and short approach established, the athlete jumps from the hop foot directly onto the strong foot for two even phases. This drill can give advanced jumpers a chance to work on the middle phase. Because the drill involves a short approach and only two phases, jumpers can do more repetitions of this drill than some other triple jump work. They should work up to doing 15 total repetitions of the drill.

High Jump

The goal of the high jump is to leap off one foot and clear a crossbar. Each jumper has three tries to get over the bar. After all competitors have either made it or missed three times, the bar is raised an inch or two. The process is continued until the last jumper misses three times. The high jump area consists of an apron for the approach run, a foam landing surface, standards, and a crossbar (see figure 9.13). The apron is usually located in the rounded D-shaped area inside the curves of a track. The wide-open area allows jumpers to approach the crossbar from a variety of angles.

The high jump is part of the Junior Olympics program for every age group. Some children are quite natural at jumping over a crossbar for height. Others can jump well but really struggle to learn the fundamental moves of crossbar clearance. Natural jumping ability does not always lead to success. Children with jumping ability and potential should be encouraged to continue practicing because the event is quite technical. Mastery of the fundamentals can take some time and patience.

The high jump poses some unique safety issues. The primary concern is to land safely as close as possible to the middle of the foam pit. Landing close to the middle is important so that the athlete does not accidentally roll off the side of the landing surface. To ensure a safe landing, the athlete needs to have a consistent takeoff position. Jumping from the wrong spot can cause the athlete to miss the pit or land too close to the edge. The uprights, or standards, used to support the crossbar are also a safety concern. An incorrect takeoff position can cause an athlete to hit the standards while jumping or landing. Finally, the bar itself can be a concern. When athletes jump at crossbars that are significantly higher than their ability will allow them to clear, they can knock the bar off with their back in such a way that causes them to land on the bar. This can be painful and even cause injuries. The solution is to jump over crossbars at heights that are challenging but reasonable. When athletes barely hit the bar with their legs or feet, the bar falls straight down onto the ground and not onto the landing area.

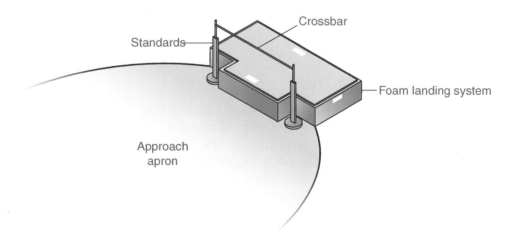

Figure 9.13   High jump area.

Scissors High Jump

As your athletes begin to learn high jump technique, the "scissors" should be used as a training tool to emphasize vertical lift. Many jumpers use the scissors as part of the warm-up on competition day. To introduce the scissors high jump, set up a jumping station on a grass field with two low uprights and a soft crossbar. Hurdles or chairs will work as uprights, and tape or an elastic band will work as a crossbar. Athletes use a short approach (no more than 15 feet), coming in at a 45-degree angle. The curved approach is not necessary for the scissors style.

The takeoff spot for the jump is about a foot away from the bar, slightly toward the near standard. The bar clearance technique involves kicking the free leg out while jumping off the outside leg. As the body clears the bar, the athlete kicks out the jumping leg as the free leg begins going down (the legs alternate like a pair of scissors). For this activity, jumpers must land on their feet. Start with the bar quite low (2 feet) and have athletes do a number of attempts from both sides (jumping off each foot). Raise the bar 6 inches or 20 centimeters at a time. The best jumpers in third and fourth grades will be able to jump over 4 feet and land relatively in control on two feet (note that this is higher than the champion at many youth meets using the flop style). Most children will start hitting the crossbar at 3 feet.

After practicing the scissors every other day for a couple of weeks, athletes can move over to the high jump pit and add the curved run instead of the diagonal approach. In combination with the curved run, jumping off the outside foot almost naturally becomes the back layout style (as described in the next section). Through observation and coaching cues, you should ensure that the athletes continue to jump—athletes need to lift their hips by pushing hard into the ground with the takeoff foot. When using the back layout, or the flop, bar clearance happens during flight, not takeoff.

High Jump Technique

The high jump technique that most people are familiar with is the Fosbury flop, or back layout. Even people with little exposure to track and field have a sense of this technique. The technique can be broken into three phases: the J-shaped approach run, the takeoff, and the flight and bar clearance.

J-Shaped Approach Run

The path of the approach run for the high jump is shaped like the letter J, meaning that it includes straight and curved portions. Note that a developmentally appropriate approach run will have only 10 total foot contacts—half on the straight portion and half on the curve. The straight portion of the approach run is used for acceleration. The jumper begins in a balanced, crouched starting position with the jumping foot forward and most of the weight on the front foot. The arms are in an alternate position with the legs. The first acceleration steps are directly forward as the athlete attempts to build momentum.

Halfway through the approach, the jumper begins the curved portion of the approach run. The transition to the curved portion should be very smooth. Many athletes have the tendency to plant the outside foot and run toward the pit at an angle, which is incorrect technique. Instead, the athlete should envision the curved portion of the run as a quarter of a circle with a 9- to 12-foot radius. Youth athletes should keep the curved portion of their approach within 12 feet; running too wide of a curve does not allow stored energies to develop that are necessary for the flight rotations. Athletes should be running at their maximum controllable speed for the jump at the beginning of the curve. Accelerating on the curve disrupts the posture and makes it difficult to be accurate at takeoff. The focus during the curved run is on maintaining a tall posture, with the hips directly under the upper body and head and with the chest facing the direction of the run. Some children turn their back slightly toward the bar during the last part of the run. This is unnecessary if the jumper is leaning into the curve because the stored rotational energy will cause the athlete to rotate in the air.

Some children might prefer a slightly longer or shorter approach. For example, for a 10-step approach, children will begin 35 to 45 feet away from the pit and about 9 to 12 feet out from the takeoff spot. One way of establishing the starting point is to do a trial run from a set point without jumping. The coach sets a mark on the approach apron at 40 feet from the pit and 10 feet out from the takeoff spot. The athlete then runs through the approach without jumping. The coach counts 5 foot contacts of the jumping leg. This will make an approach of 10 total steps, half on the straight portion of the run and half on the curve. Adjustments are made for each athlete to determine the correct starting point. Larger and stronger athletes may have to move back; smaller athletes might have to move forward.

Takeoff

The takeoff spot is located in a position that will establish a flight path that puts the jumper over the middle of the bar for a safe landing in the pit. For youth athletes jumping heights of 5 feet or more, this position is about one arm's length away from the bar and 1 to 2 feet toward the middle of the bar from the near upright. For more advanced jumpers, the takeoff spot needs to be moved out and back. For beginners, the spot needs to be moved slightly toward the middle of the bar. Caution: The takeoff spot should never be at the middle of the crossbar because the flight path will end too close to the far edge of the landing surface.

The jumping mechanics at takeoff include an aggressive drive of the free, or inside, leg. This leg drive is demonstrated by lifting the knee quickly upward past the hips while the inside arm leads up in a coordinated action with the free leg. Athletes do not need to point their back to the crossbar because this rotation will happen naturally. If the jumper leans into the curve, rotation about the hips and the long axis of the body will occur.

Flight and Bar Clearance

As previously mentioned, in the last part of the approach run, the athlete must lean into a curved running path. When the athlete jumps out of this curve, the jumper's body automatically rotates; therefore, the athlete can focus on getting the hips up over the bar. In flight, the jumper lifts the hips upward above the bar

(see figure 9.14), which is not to be confused with an arch of the back. Indeed, many jumpers keep a relatively straight back. What looks like an "arch" is an overall drape of the body from the head to the feet. Aggressively trying to arch the back causes many athletes to push their hips down into the crossbar, whereas driving the hips *up* over the crossbar is the essence of proper technique for bar clearance. The lower legs and feet drape below the bar as the hips reach the apex of the jump. As the hips cross the bar, the jumper tucks the chin against the chest, causing the lower legs to lift up and out of the way of the crossbar. The overall body rotation about the hips should cause the athlete to land on the upper back or shoulders.

Figure 9.14   Flight for the high jump.

High Jump Activities

Children training for the high jump should be exposed to a diverse range of activities that work to develop the whole athlete. In technical events such as this, coaches and athletes tend to want to do a lot of practice of the full technique that will be used in competition. In other words, they want to spend the majority of training time doing the actual high jump. However, for success in competition, athletes must be fit, must develop speed and jumping ability, and must have a sound understanding of the basic fundamentals of the approach run, takeoff, and bar clearance. Limiting practice to repeated efforts in the high jump is not the best way to develop young jumpers. Keep the training for children as general and fun as possible while still teaching the fundamentals of the technique.

SOMERSAULTS

Many people may think that somersaults—the basic gymnastics move—should be familiar to most children. However, you may be surprised to learn that many children have had little exposure to the skill and are initially unable to do it. A common reason is inflexibility in the lower back or the inability to feel comfortable in a rounded spine position. The high jump landing creates a rounded spine position, so you should provide opportunities for athletes to loosen the muscles in their back. Somersaults are a good way to loosen those muscles. You can use creativity and put numerous variations of the somersault into the warm-up routine or the activities for recovery days. Athletes can roll forward, backward, and over the shoulder. Advanced athletes will enjoy taking a running jump into a somersault on the landing area of the high jump pit. A specific program of somersaulting moves is not necessary. Activities that involve a rounded spine position can be fun and organic.

CIRCLE RUNS WITH POP-UPS

On the high jump apron, mark out a circle using cones or chalk. The radius of the circle should be about 10 feet or 3 meters. Athletes run around the circle, focusing on posture. The athletes lean to the middle of the circle from the ankles. On a command or at a designated spot in the circle, the athletes jump up off the inside foot. The coach and the athlete will notice that the flight causes an automatic rotation about the long axis (the length of the body). If rotation does not occur, it is likely that the athlete came out of the curve (stopped leaning into the middle) immediately before takeoff. Progressively working up to three sets of 10 runs and pop-ups would be sufficient volume for this drill.

SHORT-APPROACH HIGH JUMP

Much of the technical work involved in the mechanics of takeoff and bar clearance can be taught using short approaches. The short approach limits the amount of speed an athlete can develop during the run-up. This reduces the amount of force an athlete can generate at takeoff. Because of this, more repetitions can be attempted before significant fatigue develops.

Short approaches typically include three or five foot contacts. For these drills, the entire approach happens on the curve. To establish the starting position for the three-step approach, athletes can take three giant steps back from the desired takeoff spot. Stronger athletes may have to move a foot or two farther back after taking the three giant steps. To establish the starting position for a five-step approach, athletes should do a "run-back" of their approach. To do this, they simply begin from their takeoff spot and run back five steps, completing the run with a pop-up. After athletes have established effective starting points for their short-approach runs, you should have the athletes record the measurements for future practices.

BOX JUMPS

This would be considered an advanced drill. Children of all ages can be successful at jumping off of low boxes. However, only children who have gained significant mastery of the approach run, takeoff, bar clearance, and landing should attempt this drill. Many athletes find that jumping off low boxes can be very helpful. A stable and sturdy box is placed at the takeoff spot. The box should have a base that is a minimum of 2 feet by 3 feet and should be no taller than 6 inches. Ideally, the surface of the box will be the same as the track, but wood and glued-down carpet can also work. Buy a commercially available product if possible.

Athletes should use short approaches for this drill. Having the takeoff 6 inches higher has a couple of effects that will increase the result of the jump. The obvious advantage is that the athlete's center of mass will be elevated at takeoff. In addition, the athlete's takeoff leg will be loaded to a greater degree because of the box. In other words, the slightly higher takeoff spot increases the bend at the knee and hip, allowing for a greater expression of force.

Pole Vault

The pole vault area includes a linear runway, a plant box, a foam landing surface, standards, and a crossbar (see figure 9.15). In this event, jumpers use a pole to swing over a crossbar that is raised at a predetermined progression. Jumpers have three attempts at each height. The athlete who clears the highest height is the winner.

The pole vault is part of the Junior Olympics program starting with the youth division for both boys and girls. Clearly, the event is one of the most technically challenging events in track and field. It also demands significant athletic ability. Successful vaulters must have sprinter speed, good spring, upper body and trunk strength, and acrobatic talent. Successful vaulters also have to be disciplined and coachable. Because the equipment is very expensive and the event is obviously dangerous, an athlete must demonstrate the potential to develop the required attributes in order to pursue the event.

Pole Vault Technique

Learning how to pole vault is a time-consuming process. Athletes need to gain an understanding of the basic fundamentals and demonstrate proficiency before attempting to vault for height. The basic fundamentals include the grip, the approach run, the pole plant and jump, and finally, the swing to an inverted position and bar clearance.

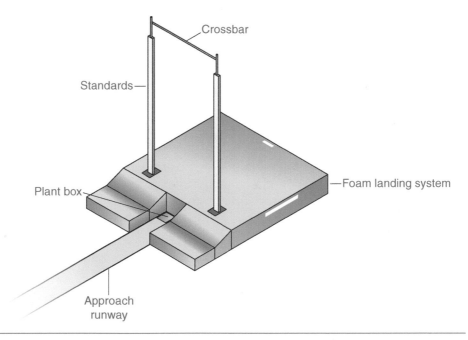

Figure 9.15   Pole vault area.

Pole Vault Grip

The proper grip enables the athlete to (1) control the pole while developing speed on the runway, (2) effectively plant the pole, and (3) hold onto the pole through the phases of the vault. For right-handed vaulters, the right hand is held in the top position, and the hands are typically held about shoulder-width apart. To establish the proper grip, athletes should simulate the plant position by holding both arms straight up while pushing the top of the pole up with the palms of their hands (see figure 9.16*a*). From this position, the athletes bring the top hand down to the hip and hold the bottom hand about chest height out in front of the body (see figure 9.16*b*). This action raises up the bottom end of the pole for the run. Athletes should practice jogging and then running with the pole to develop control and a level of comfort.

Grip height (how high the top hand is located on the pole) is an important consideration that should never be approached haphazardly. Beginning vaulters can practice running with the pole while using a high hand grip. However, when actual plants and jumps become part of the practice, a low grip height is essential. To establish a starting point for novice vaulters, have them stand next to the pole and reach up. Six inches above standing reach is a conservative grip height for the first few drills involving a plant and jump. As the athletes safely perform the drill, the grip height can be slowly moved up one hand width (or half a hand width) at a time. Many coaches mark 4-inch intervals on the pole with a permanent marker to help ensure that athletes always have the intended grip height.

Pole Vault Safety

Pole vaulting consistently and safely takes great expertise, and developing this expertise takes time, dedication, and patience. Essentially, the starting point for this event is an absolute commitment to safety in all aspects ranging from maintaining equipment to teaching proper technique. Here are some tips to help you maintain safety in the pole vault:

- Monitor how high athletes' hands are positioned on the pole. Athletes should begin with a grip height no higher than 6 inches above their reach on the pole (when standing next to the pole). As athletes successfully complete drills, they can slowly raise their handhold.
- Never let athletes use cracked or chipped poles. The weakness caused from the cracks could cause the poles to break when the athlete is jumping.
- Store poles properly. They should be stored in a safe place where only coaches have access. Do not leave poles in an unheated shed during the winter because the freeze-thaw cycle can break down the fiberglass material.
- Remind athletes not to lay poles flat on the ground during meets or practice. This will help prevent the poles from getting stepped on.
- Make sure the foam landing surface meets regulations and is in good condition.
- Make sure all practices are conducted under the supervision of a trained coach.
- Do not allow athletes to vault in bad weather (excessive rain, wind, and so on).

Pole Vault Approach

For the approach, the athlete's goal is to develop maximum controllable speed while putting the body and the pole in a jumping position at the end of the run. To accomplish this task, athletes should use 12 to 16 total steps (6 to 8 contacts with the takeoff foot) in their approach. The approach can be divided into three phases: acceleration, middle, and transition to jump. These phases are similar to those described previously for the long jump (see page 120).

The first acceleration steps are characterized by big, strong pushes down the runway that are deliberate and aggressive. Athletes should avoid jogging into the approach; this can create inconsistency and cause the jumper to feel the need to accelerate late in the run. By the middle of the run, maximum controllable speed has been developed, and the jumper focuses on running

a   b

Figure 9.16   Establishing proper grip for the pole vault.

tall with good posture and balance (which resembles the mechanics of sprinting at maximum velocity).

Four steps out from the plant, the athlete begins the transition from running and building up momentum to planting the pole and jumping off the runway surface. Some people refer to this phase as the "pole drop." During the acceleration and middle phases of the run, the pole is held upright (see figure 9.17). During the transition, the athlete lowers the tip of the pole. Good timing of this pole drop is demonstrated by having the hands above the head and having the tip of the pole aimed at the plant box during the penultimate step. As the tip of the pole lowers to the ground, the athlete's hands must stay in front of the body. Many athletes have a tendency to move the top hand behind the hip to help control the pole drop. This twists the shoulders out of alignment and into a dangerous position for planting the pole.

As a coach, you will need to teach beginners the transition phase by having them practice many approach runs and plants on the track. First, work with athletes to establish a starting point that will be used consistently so that you and the athlete can begin to learn how long the approach should be. After consistency is developed, place a target (such as a towel or a box drawn with chalk) on the track to represent the plant box. Hitting the target with the pole tip at the end of the run is a prerequisite to any advanced drills or actual jumps into the pit.

Figure 9.17   Acceleration phase for the pole vault.

Pole Plant

The pole plant is considered by many to be the most important part of the pole vault. Inaccuracy and inconsistency can lead to big problems. Investing significant training time into perfecting the plant is a wise decision. Key elements of a good pole plant are the jumping position, the angle between the runway and the pole, and the accuracy and consistency of the takeoff.

Jumping Position   A common problem that youth athletes have in the pole vault is swinging under the pole without actually jumping to push the pole up at takeoff. Jumping at the plant is essential, and the mechanics are similar to those for the long jump. Right-handed vaulters will jump off of their left leg, meaning that the right leg will take the penultimate step (see figure 9.18*a*). A subtle lowering of the hips occurs in this position to prepare for vertical lift. When the body is over the right foot in this last support step, the pole must already be raised from the hip, and the athlete's palms should be facing up (see figure 9.18*b*). At this point, the end of the pole is pointing toward the plant box. The vaulter pushes off of the penultimate step into the takeoff step (see figure 9.18*c*). At this point, the pole is aggressively pushed up, and the left leg pushes down and back, causing the jump.

Angle Between the Runway and the Pole   The primary goal in the pole vault is to get the pole to a vertical position so the vaulter can swing over a

a   b   c

Figure 9.18   Proper positioning for the pole plant.

crossbar. To get the pole to a vertical position most efficiently, the athlete must start with a tall plant. A tall plant means that the top hand is directly over the takeoff foot. There should be an active effort to push the top of the pole up. Pulling down on the top of the pole to create bend is a common error and is extremely dangerous. The pole should be pushed up with both hands very aggressively at the takeoff. The energy from the run will create bend in the pole as the vaulter begins to swing on the pole.

Accuracy and Consistency of the Takeoff   An accurate takeoff position is critical. Vaulters will have trouble clearing the crossbar if their takeoff position is too close to the pit (called "being under") or too far away from the pit (called "being out"). Being under can be caused by having an approach run that is too long. However, being under is most often caused by having a late plant—that is, the athlete did not get the hands up and the pole tip down by the penultimate step. When this occurs, the pole has to move from the hip to the position above the head during the movement into the jump. Getting the pole into this position takes time, and the takeoff leg floats out before making contact, causing the athlete to be under. To fix the under step, the athlete needs to have an earlier plant. A takeoff position that is too far out is likely caused by an inaccurate approach run. Either the distance is wrong or the rhythm and consistency of the approach phases are off. In this case, the athlete needs to go back to the track and practice runway rehearsals with plants into a towel until consistency is developed.

Inversion and Bar Clearance

As the athlete leaves the ground, the body stays long and swings from the top hand. The athlete attempts to maintain this long swing to create penetration. When the body stays long through the swing, the center of mass of the pole–athlete system is lowered, causing the pole to move to a vertical position more efficiently. A common error is rocking back into an inverted position too early. This raises the center of mass of the system, causing the pole to slow down and fail to get to a vertical position. Cues such as "stay long" and "sweep the trail leg low" can help athletes learn to be patient and keep the body long during the swing.

At the end of the first swing, the athlete uses the abdominal muscles and the muscles of the upper back to pull himself into an upside-down position. During this phase, the head stays in natural alignment with the spine. Bringing the knees to the hands takes significant strength. Many young vaulters "flag" (i.e., fail to get inverted) because they lack development in the trunk and upper back.

From the inverted position, the jumper pulls the hands to the chest and then pushes down on the pole as he lifts the hips into the air. During this pull, right-handed vaulters will rotate toward their right so that they will face the bar during clearance. For some vaulters, this happens quite naturally. Others need to really concentrate on turning while pulling. Pointing the right toe inward can help start the rotation.

Leading with the feet, the athlete pikes, or bends at the waist, as the body clears the bar. The final push off the pole is done with the top hand. This push helps the upper body and the arms clear the bar. Good vaulters maintain excellent awareness as they fly freely in the air. Athletes should try to land on their backs in the middle of the pit. Novice vaulters often attempt to land on their feet. This should be discouraged because the ankles and knees can be injured landing on the unstable surface.

Pole Vault Activities

Once they have begun to master the fundamentals of the event, some athletes have a tendency to exclusively practice actual pole vaulting. However, you should ensure that young athletes maintain a general approach to training for as long as possible. Even advanced adolescents would do well to invest the majority of training time in developing speed, strength, power, and detailed aspects of technique. As these attributes improve, so will performance in competitions. Much of the training for the pole vault will be similar to that of jumpers or sprinters. This works well for a youth track team because a significant portion of the training for individual events can be done in larger groups. About a third of the training should be event specific. This section provides ideas for some activities that can be used to train for the pole vault.

SAND PIT JUMPS

This drill is a fun introduction to the event and can be used for more advanced jumpers to work on specific aspects of the plant. It can also be used to reinforce the long swing from the top hand. From a short run, the athlete plants and swings into the long jump pit. At no point does the athlete attempt to go upside down. The body stays upright, and the jumper swings on the side of the pole (a right-handed jumper will swing on the right side of the pole) and lands carefully in the sand. The jumper lands on the feet. The top arm remains straight, and the bottom arm bends as the body passes the pole.

BARS AND RINGS

The high bars and rings located on playgrounds can be used to work on the upper body and abdominal strength needed for the event. If athletes cannot support their body weight on the high bar, they should not be pole vaulting. Fundamental moves include bringing the knees to the elbows while leaving the arms straight. A more advanced move would be to bring the knees up past the elbows and lift the hips above the head. This simulates the swing to an inverted position.

POLE RUNS

Pole vault rehearsals on the track are an important part of the training program for vaulters, teaching them how to swing on the pole and land safely on both feet. These can be done in a number of different ways. A general approach would be practicing on short runways in training shoes, which can be done by marking a "plant box" on the track surface with tape or chalk to use as a target. Remember, the approach run while wearing training shoes will likely be slightly shorter than while wearing spikes.

There are many activities that can be performed at the pole vault pit to gain strength and learn technique. Two are:

- *One-handed swings.* Because it takes two hands to plant the pole, this drill starts with the jumper pushing the pole down the runway with the tip of the pole rubbing against the surface. When the pole hits the back of the box, the vaulter pushes up with the top hand and swings into the pit. The bottom hand is held out for balance.

Coaching Tip

Using the proper equipment is essential in this event. In every case, athletes should jump using the shortest pole possible for their developmental level. Athletes should never use a pole that is too soft. Here are some guidelines to help you understand pole selection:

- Too much penetration—use a higher hand grip

- Too much bend—use a stiffer pole or lower the hand grip

- Penetration too shallow—use a lower hand grip

- *Rock backs.* For this drill, athletes use a short approach and a low hand-hold. The first swing is followed by an aggressive rock back into the inverted position. The drill ends there, and the athlete lands on her back while still holding onto the pole. Essentially, this move is the first part of the vault without the pull and turn out of the inverted position.

HORIZONTAL VAULTING

This fundamental move might be familiar to children and adults from rural environments. Essentially, this activity involves jumping for distance rather than for height. A short pole and a short approach area on a soft grass field are needed. The pole should be 2 meters in length. Leave both ends of the pole open. Leaving the end plug off of the bottom of the pole will allow the pole to grab into the grass surface more securely. On the top of the pole, place five strips of colored tape at 6-inch intervals starting 6 inches from the top. The coach uses the tape to carefully monitor and control the height of the hand grip. Athletes should use the lowest grip possible and should raise the grip 3 inches at a time only when they have mastered safe landings. Mastery is demonstrated by landing safely on two feet. The approach area can be marked by placing cones on the grass field. The approach run should be no longer than 10 meters. A hula hoop is placed flat on the grass at the end of the run and serves as the location to plant the pole.

10

Coaching the Throws

The throwing events for youth track and field test the athletes' coordination and explosive power. The primary objective in these events is to achieve maximum distance. However, accuracy is also important because the implements must land in a designated impact area. Teaching children how to throw far requires an understanding of key fundamentals as well as specific techniques. In this chapter, we begin by providing information on basic mechanics that are common to all the throwing events. Then, we discuss technical aspects and developmental considerations for each specific event.

See table 10.1 for a list of the throwing events for each age group for both the USATF Junior Olympics and the Hershey's Track & Field Games.

Table 10.1

USATF Junior Olympics	
Bantam (ages 10 and under)	Shot put (6 lb), javelin throw (300 g)
Midget (ages 11 and 12)	Shot put (6 lb), discus throw (1 kg), javelin throw (300 g)
Youth (ages 13 and 14)	Shot put (6 lb for girls / 4 kg for boys), discus throw (1 kg), javelin throw (600 g)
Intermediate (ages 15 and 16)	Shot put (4 kg for girls / 12 lb for boys), discus throw (1 kg for girls / 1.6 kg for boys), javelin throw (600 g for girls/800 g for boys), hammer throw
Young (ages 17 and 18)	Shot put (4 kg for young women / 12 lb for young men), discus throw (1 kg for young women / 1.6 kg for young men), javelin throw (600 g for young women / 800 g for young men), hammer throw
Hershey's Track & Field Games	
Ages 9 and 10	Softball throw
Ages 11 and 12	Softball throw
Ages 13 and 14	Softball throw

General Throwing Mechanics

Athletes and coaches who seriously pursue the throwing events will consider every possible idea that mght improve performance. And while it is beneficial to take the time to closely analyze technique, coaches working with children just learning how to throw should consider teaching the fundamentals before focusing too heavily on the minor details. It is true that each of the throws—shot put, discus, javelin, hammer, and softball—has unique qualities, but some general mechanical principles apply to all of them as well. At every developmental level, from novice to elite, the coach and athlete both need to understand these principles so that instruction and training can be more efficient to help throwers reach their potential.

Throwing Event Safety

For the throwing events, safety is the most important thing for coaches, parents, officials, and athletes to consider. Some of the implements used for these events evolved from ancient instruments of war—thus, they were originally designed to do damage to property and people. Everybody must work together to ensure that the throwing environment is safe. Here are some guidelines to follow with your athletes:

- Ensure that all throwing practices are supervised.
- Make sure that throwing is done from a legal throwing area or cage during practice and competitions (as specified for the respective events later in this chapter).
- Teach all your athletes that they should never turn their backs to the throwing area.
- During throwing practice, have all athletes throw and then go together to retrieve their implements after everybody has thrown.
- Instruct everyone to be aware of and to watch for bounces because implements can cause injury. People must not get too close to the implements as they land.
- Do not allow horseplay during throwing practices or competitions. Everybody has to pay attention at all times.
- Make sure that people do not stand too close to the person throwing. For all events, people must stay at least 10 feet behind the thrower.
- Teach your athletes that they should not leave implements unattended. All equipment should be stored in a secure place when your athletes are done training or competing.
- Educate nonthrowers on safety issues. Make sure that the runners are aware of the impact areas so that they do not accidentally run into danger.

Parabolic Curve

How far something will travel after being thrown can be determined by three mathematical variables: height of release, speed of release, and angle of release. Measurements of these variables can be calculated to determine the flight path—or parabolic curve—of the implement. Aerodynamic factors also come into play, especially in the discus and javelin. In addition, the effect of wind will clearly alter the parabolic curve. Ideas on how your athletes can use those aerodynamic factors to their advantage will be discussed in more detail in the sections for each specific event later in this chapter. Here, we briefly discuss the basics for the height, speed, and angle of release.

Height of Release

In the throwing events, athletes should make every effort to maximize the height of release. This is done largely by "staying tall" and having good posture at the end of the throw. A common mistake made by young athletes is called "breaking at the hips," where the athlete bends at the hips and waist rather than standing tall at the point of release. It takes a certain level of strength to be able to maintain posture while releasing an implement. Therefore, you will need to be patient with your athletes and work with them to develop core stability and strength in order to improve this aspect of their technique.

Speed of Release

The speed of the implement at the point of release is perhaps the most obvious variable that comes into play during throwing events. Rhythmic acceleration is essential for the implement to be moving fast at the point of release. Young athletes often make the mistake of starting too fast and are then unable to accelerate near the release. Teach your athletes to slow it down at the beginning in favor of rhythmically accelerating for the fastest possible throw.

Angle of Release

The angle of release will vary by implement and by the strength and ability of the athlete. For maximum distance, the optimal angle of release for a projectile is 45 degrees. So, no throw should be released at an angle greater than that. Remember, we are measuring for distance, not for height. For some athletes, it can be advantageous to have a significantly lower release—perhaps as low as 30 degrees. For example, shorter javelin and hammer throwers might hit the ground with the implement if they create too steep of a release angle. Strength levels also need to be considered. Young shot-putters might have difficulty creating a big lift at the end of the throw and might have better results using a flatter release. As a general rule, a proper release angle on long throws (discus, javelin, softball, and hammer) is within the range of 27 to 38 degrees, and a proper release angle for the shot put is from 32 to 40 degrees.

Summate Force

To maximize their potential to create high release speed, throwers must generate a summate force, which means that the firing of each muscle is coordinated to optimize speed and force production. Summate force is a good example of the old saying "The whole is greater than the sum of the parts." During a throw, one movement should set up the next so that the implement is moving fast during the final part of the throw. For example, the hand and arm can only throw a discus so far. But, the discus will fly considerably farther when an athlete first gets the discus moving with the legs and the trunk and then adds an appropriately timed arm strike at the end.

Range Throwing for Training

In every throwing event, the goal is to achieve maximum distance. Therefore, it is only natural that athletes frequently want to attempt all-out throws in practice. However, this is not the best way for your athletes to improve. To work on technique and achieve more volume, progressive loading is necessary over the long term. *Progressive loading* is the term coaches use to describe the systematic increase in training demand over time. Too much volume or intensity early in a training cycle can lead to injury. A broad base of training that includes a gradual increase in demand over the course of several months will allow athletes to reach higher peaks toward the end of the season. Therefore, partial throws or submaximal efforts are an important part of the training program.

When designing a training program, you should first have the athlete establish a baseline of maximum effort. Once the athlete's personal best is known, you can determine various levels of less intense trials. For example, if an athlete's best throw in competition (or in training if the athlete is a beginner) is 100 feet in the discus or the softball throw, you can set a cone at 75 feet and have the athlete practice 15 to 20 throws at this distance. This is referred to as *three-fourths effort*. For personal bests that are not 100 feet, the coach might have to use some math to determine the appropriate range. The idea is that for athletes to really throw with full intensity, they need a base of solid technical work and volume. If every throw in practice is a maximum effort, performance plateaus will set in, and the idea of maximum effort will get watered down.

The following chart can be used as a guideline for designing training plans using the concept of range throwing. The high end of the volume range listed represents the potential of a well-prepared athlete after several weeks of progressive loading.

	Medium (extensive)	High (intensive)	Competitive (explosive)
% of personal best	70-80	80-90	>90
# of throws	30-50	10-20	<10
# of sessions per week	2-3	1-2	1-2

In the throwing events, the general principle for the summation of forces is that the big muscles should fire first, the medium-size muscles next, and the small muscles last. For example, in the shot put, the athlete pushes first with the legs and hips, then adds rotation of the trunk to get the shot moving even faster before the arm strike, and finally flicks the implement off the fingertips using the muscles of the wrist.

Shoulder–Hip Separation (Torque)

Although shoulder–hip separation, or torque, must be timed appropriately to fit into the generation of a summate force (as previously discussed), torque can also be considered as a specific aspect of the mechanics of throwing. In each of the throws, the shoulder–hip separation is critical for the recruitment and use of the muscles in the trunk. For example, imagine a line connecting the two points on the side of the hips and another line connecting the two shoulders. When an athlete is standing or sitting naturally, these two lines are parallel. Torque occurs when these two lines shift out of the parallel position because of rotation of the spine, or long axis of the body. This separation of the shoulders and the hips prestretches the muscles of the trunk. If this separation is timed correctly in the execution of a throw, these stretched muscles contract, causing the upper body to rotate about the long axis and accelerate the implement.

Blocking

In relation to throwing, *blocking* refers to bracing one side of the body so that the other side can move quickly and forcefully. This action takes advantage of the physics of *angular momentum.* Basically, angular momentum describes how the rotational momentum in a moving system (in this case, a thrower and an implement) is transferred when part of the system gets suddenly stopped. For example, imagine what happens when a person slams on the brakes in a car or hits the front brakes on a bike. The stuff in the backseat flies forward in the car, and the bicycle rider might fly over the handlebars of the bike.

To apply angular momentum to the throws, athletes brace one side and let the other side whip around. For example, a right-handed thrower will brace the left side. To initiate the brace, or block, the thrower establishes firm foot contact with the throwing surface. Then, the athlete creates a strong and stable left side—from the foot to the shoulder—to allow the right side to accelerate with the implement.

Softball Throw

The softball throw is an event in Hershey's Track & Field Games. Simply stated, the fundamental move used in this event is the same overhand throwing technique that children learn when throwing softballs and baseballs.

Indeed, the ball used for all age groups in the Hershey program is a standard-size softball: 6 ounces with a 12-inch circumference. The main difference in the softball throw for track and field is that accuracy is less important than in baseball or softball because the distance is measured in a 50-foot-wide landing area. This allows athletes to focus on trying to maximize the height of release and on putting their energy into throwing as far as they can. See figure 10.1 for an example of the field layout for the softball throw.

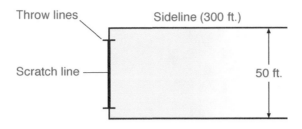

Figure 10.1   Softball throw area.

The importance of safety must not be underestimated just because the implement is called a "soft" ball. Even though the ball is relatively light, it can cause injury. The overhand throwing motion used in this event can lead to injuries of the shoulders or elbows if athletes throw too much or throw with poor form. And, as discussed previously, to reduce the potential for injury, athletes should not throw for maximum distance at the beginning of the season (or at the beginning of your practices, for that matter). You may find that many of your athletes will want to try to throw all out too early in the season or the practice session. This can be dangerous if the athlete has not done much throwing, because the small muscles of the shoulder will be highly taxed. As a coach, you need to design your practices to help prevent these injuries. For example, you can set up cones on the field at a reasonable distance and have the children throw 10 to 20 balls. For each training session, you should make sure that your athletes warm up with some loosening moves and some submaximal throwing. Another way that you can help reduce the chance of injury is to limit your athletes' throwing to every other day (at the most) in order to allow for recovery.

Softball Throw Technique

The rules in the Hershey program allow athletes to throw the softball from a standing position or with a short run-up. Most children will use a run-up in competition. However, learning the standing throw is part of the developmental process. By first practicing the softball throw without a run-up, the athletes can learn to throw with their hips and trunk and learn how to use a safe overhead throwing action. After the athletes achieve some consistency with the standing throw, short running approaches can be added.

Standing Softball Throw

When first teaching your athletes how to properly throw a ball for distance, you can begin by teaching them the softball throw without a run-up (also called the *standing softball throw*).

Grip   The first thing to consider for a standing throw is the grip. The ball should rest comfortably at the base of the fingers, contacting very little of the

Figure 10.2   Proper grip for the softball throw.

palm (see figure 10.2). The thumb, ring finger, and pinky finger support the outside of the ball. The index and middle fingers are behind the ball.

Stance   For the standing softball throw, the athlete starts with the body facing a quarter turn away from the target (see figure 10.3). The hand that is holding the ball will be farthest away from the direction of the throw. The athlete should stand tall with the feet facing straight ahead or rotated slightly toward the target. The arms and shoulders are held in a loose posture.

Figure 10.3   Initial stance for the standing softball throw.

Windup   To get ready to throw from the initial stance, the athlete moves the nonthrowing arm toward the direction of the throw to help maintain balance while pulling the hand with the ball back as far from the target as possible (see figure 10.4). The palm should face up in the last part of the windup.

Upper- and Lower-Body Action   To initiate the throw, the athlete shifts her weight forward and rotates the hips in the direction of the throw (see figure 10.5). While rotating the hips, the athlete needs to be patient with the upper body and leave the ball back until the hips are facing the throwing direction. The upper-body movement of the throw will happen naturally if a stretch has been created with the advanced hip movement. The throwing arm moves into an overhead

Figure 10.4   Windup for the standing soft-ball throw.

Figure 10.5   Upper- and lower-body action for the standing softball throw.

throwing action and stays high above the shoulder while the opposite side of the body braces to allow a strong throw.

Follow-Through   After the ball is released, the throwing arm continues down and across the body. The athlete bends at the waist and uses the muscles of the trunk to slow down and stop the throwing action.

Softball Throw With a Run-Up

The basic grip and mechanics of the softball throw with a run-up are the same as for the standing softball throw (as discussed previously). The main objective of using a run-up is to build up some momentum to increase the overall distance thrown. When using a run-up, the two major differences from the standing throw are the windup and the follow-through. Also, the lower body action is slightly more difficult to time when using a run-up than when performing a standing throw.

Windup   For the softball throw with a run-up, coordinating the withdrawal of the ball with the forward movement of the feet is more difficult than execut-ing the windup for a standing throw. Getting into the windup position while on the run may take a bit of practice for your young athletes. The arm action is the same in both styles. The footwork for the windup is similar to the crow hop in baseball and softball. Many children will be able to do this move naturally because of their experiences with other sports, but others may need to be taught the technique. For right-handed throwers, the crow hop consists of an elongated stride with the right leg during the windup. This elongated stride allows time for the ball to get back before the left leg lands.

Upper- and Lower-Body Action   The key to throwing far from a standing position is to be patient and use the lower body to initiate the movement. With a running start, the whole body is already moving forward, so getting the hips into the throw is more difficult. Again, the key is to be patient and allow the hips to rotate forward while leaving the arm back. The end of the run should result in a throwing stance that allows the hips to rotate forward. Athletes should start with slow runs and add speed only when they can do the throwing technique properly.

Follow-Through   As mentioned, one of the other major differences between the standing softball throw and the softball throw with a run-up is the follow-through. Athletes need to allow enough room from the scratch line for a fairly large follow-through step. For a right-handed thrower, the left leg will block, and the right side will whip into the throw. Even for the smallest children, this should be so aggressive that the right foot has to step forward in the follow-through. The athlete's size and speed will determine how far back from the scratch line the left foot should be planted. For most athletes, 5 feet would be a good starting point and then adjustments can be made on an individual basis.

Also note that shoulder injuries sometimes occur in the back part of the muscle as it works to slow the arm down after the release. The risk of this type of injury can be reduced by teaching athletes to have a long follow-through. A long follow-through includes complete movement of the throwing arm toward the ground and an extra step.

Coaching Tip

Many children who compete in the softball throw will also compete in other events. Therefore, the training program for throwers should include all aspects of general athletic development. Children interested in this event can do some work with the sprinters and jumpers to feel like part of the bigger team and to work on speed and explosiveness.

Softball Throw Activities

Following are several activities that you can use with your athletes when you teach the softball throw. Rather than just throwing, the training for softball throwers should involve activities that will help develop attributes that contribute to injury prevention and success in competition. Specifically, training should allow athletes to work on shoulder and elbow conditioning, the development of proper and consistent form, and the core strength and arm speed required for throwing far.

SHOULDER MOVES

Softball throwers should work on developing the shoulder by using moves that improve shoulder flexibility and stability. These moves are similar to those commonly used by baseball pitchers. Here are two examples (the local high school pitcher can probably show you many more):

- Standing upright with the elbow pointing out and the arm facing up, the athlete moves the hand down while leaving the elbow out, rotating only at the shoulder.
- Standing upright with the elbow at the side, the athlete rotates the hand back and forth, parallel with the ground.

Have your athletes start with 3 sets of 10 for each arm and increase as they gain more strength. Additionally, both of these moves can be enriched by holding the ball or a small weight, or by using elastic bands or bungee cords.

REVERSE BALL FLICKS

Athletes line up approximately 3 feet apart, facing one direction. Using a reverse throwing motion, athletes flick the ball back, away from the direction they are facing. After everyone has thrown, all the athletes can go and retrieve the balls. Start with 10 throws and build up to 20 throws each arm. This is a move that can be incorporated into the warm-up to stretch and strengthen the shoulder. Although the ball used in competition will work well and keep things simple, advanced athletes could progress to using weighted balls (up to 1 kilogram).

THROWING ROCKS

Look for places where there are many 1- to 2-inch rocks on the ground, such as a gravel parking lot or a field. Have your athletes throw rocks within the area or even into the woods or into a lake or river. For adolescents or advanced youth, 50 rock throws for distance would be an excellent and challenging activity. For beginners and young children, 25 throws at full intensity is enough. Safety should be a primary concern when conducting this activity, and athletes must never throw at targets intending to cause damage.

RUN-UP

The goal of the run-up, or approach, is to build up some momentum before the final movements of the throw. Facility constraints and meet rules will determine the specific length of the runway. Also, too much speed will make it difficult to have control at the end of the run-up. So, children should take a modest approach run of less than 50 feet (significantly shorter in some cases).

Remember, the athlete needs to release the ball approximately 5 feet from the foul line to allow space for a follow-through step.

Place cones or markers at 5-foot intervals from 25 to 50 feet. Have athletes start at the first cone, perform a run-up, and go through the throwing motion without the ball. The athletes should then move back 5 feet and try again. Work with each athlete to determine what distance is most comfortable and consistent. If the run-up causes problems with the final throw, the athlete can compete from a standing position or try a two- or three-step approach.

Shot Put

The shot put is part of the Junior Olympics program at every level. This event is popular at many meets because athletes of all shapes and sizes enjoy putting the shot. Indeed, it is a misconception that shot-putters need to be big. In youth track, the implements are actually not that heavy. Any athlete who is interested in learning the event and training with consistency can have some success in the shot. Explosive power, speed, and coordination are attributes of the top competitors.

The implement itself is called a *shot*. *Put* is the verb that describes the arm motion that distinguishes this event from a "throw." *Put* means that the implement has to travel from the shoulder directly to the point of release (rather than taking a wider, curved path to the release as in throwing a ball). The shot is made of metal and is slightly smaller than a softball. It is quite heavy relative to its size.

The event is contested in a designated area with a concrete throwing circle and a raised toe board (see figure 10.6). The throwing circle is 7 feet in diameter. The area where the shots land is generally gravel because the implements will cause damage to sport fields. This impact area is marked with a 34.92-degree sector. A fair throw lands inside the sector and is measured from the inside of the toe board to the point where the implement initially lands.

The concern for safety in this event is extreme. The heavy metal balls can cause significant injury if they accidentally strike a person. All safety precautions regarding the impact area need to be taken. Athletes can also get injured by not using proper technique. Throwing the shot instead of putting it—that is, using a curved arm path toward release rather than a linear push—is against the rules and is dangerous because it puts enormous pressure on the small muscles of the elbow and shoulder. Teach good technique and maintain a safe environment to eliminate the chance for injury.

Shot Put Technique

The basic technical elements of the shot put are the grip, arm strike, and release; the power position; and moving across the ring.

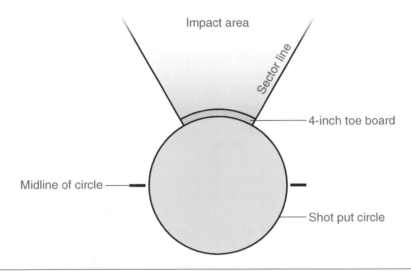

Figure 10.6   Shot put area.

Grip, Arm Strike, and Release

When teaching the shot put, you should begin with the grip, arm strike, and release. The ball is held along the base of the fingers, and the fingers should be either together or close together (see figure 10.7). A common error at the youth level is trying to grip the shot with the hand. The ball should be pressed against the neck, with the elbow out and with the pressure of the arm pressing into the neck, allowing the shot to be stable. The opposite arm is held out and kept long for balance.

For the arm strike and release, the athlete executes a complete push all the way through the fingertips. The elbow stays out during the strike, and the hand flicks away at the point of release.

Power Position

Once your athletes have a basic understanding of the grip, arm strike, and release, they can begin to use the whole body to generate force into the throw. Learning how to throw from the power position helps activate the trunk, hips, and legs into the throw. For right-handed throwers, the stance starts with the left foot near the front of the circle and the right foot

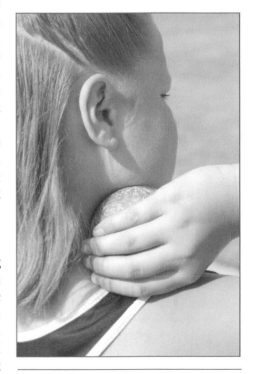

Figure 10.7   Proper grip for the shot put.

Figure 10.8   Proper stance for the power position.

back so that the feet are about shoulder-width apart (see figure 10.8). The feet are set with the toe of the front foot and the heel of the back foot lined up with the direction of the throw—called *heel–toe relationship*. This stance allows a full range of motion during the lifting and rotational phase.

Gripping the shot as previously described, the athlete squats and twists at the same time. How deep an athlete squats depends on strength, but for most children a one-quarter squat is sufficient. The athlete then twists away from the direction of the throw until the back faces the impact area. The feet must maintain stable contact with the throwing surface, and the hips should not twist back. Most of the twisting happens along the spine, with the trunk causing the rotation. Torque is established by having "open" hips and "closed" shoulders. This means that the hips are opened toward the direction of the throw while the shoulders are rotated back away from the direction of the throw.

Getting into this position causes a loading effect. The muscles that will be used to put the shot are stretched so that they are ready to contract and cause the shot to start accelerating. The key is to fire them in the right order to maximize the potential of summate force development. The wrist and fingers play an important role in the release, but they are totally ineffective unless the ball already has a good deal of momentum. Essentially, the two big forces that are generated early are the lifting potential of the legs and hips and the rotational potential of the trunk. Near the end of the lift and twist, the muscles of the chest, shoulder, and arm fire to release the shot. The left side of the body braces—or blocks—from the bottom of the foot to the shoulder, creating a hinge for the right side to whip about (see figure 10.9a). As the chest begins to face the direction of the throw, the athlete initiates the arm strike (see figure 10.9b) and the release (see figure 10.9c). At the point of release, the athlete needs to be as tall as possible. This maximizes the height of release and ensures that all the potential energy of the hips and legs has been expressed.

The angle of release is typically 32 to 40 degrees, but there is a considerable amount of variation in this. Some athletes, even at the highest levels of competition, have great success establishing flatter releases. Obviously, the implement has to get some height to travel, but there is a trade-off. If an athlete can be more aggressive and have a faster speed of release with a lesser angle, the athlete may have more success by releasing the shot at a low

Figure 10.9   Arm strike and release.

angle of about 33 degrees. The key is to have your athletes experiment and to determine what is best for each individual. Also, individual preferences will change over time. As athletes get stronger, faster, and a better command of the technique, they may be more effective with a different release angle than when they were learning the event.

Moving Across the Ring

More advanced athletes can build up even more momentum by moving across the ring (this should only be attempted after the power position has been mastered to an adequate extent). Two techniques are commonly used for moving across the ring: the glide and the spin.

Glide   For the glide technique, a right-handed athlete would begin by balancing on the right foot in the back of the ring, with the foot and the back facing away from the direction of the throw (see figure 10.10a). The movement begins with a slight "unseating" or settling back with the hips in the direction of the throw (see figure 10.10b). Just after the unseating, the athlete pushes off the throwing surface with the right foot and shoots the left foot low and aggressively toward the toe board. The right foot is pulled under the body, and both feet land together in the power position stance (see figure 10.10c).

Figure 10.10   Moving across the ring using the glide.

Two key technical points need to be considered for the glide technique. First, the glide movement has to help build up the momentum and generate a greater summate force. If that is not happening, the athlete might be better off sticking with the power position throw for a while. Second, a common mistake that athletes make when using this technique is opening their shoulders as they come out of the back of the ring. This eliminates the potential to develop torque. One way to fix this problem is to have the shot-putters use a focal point. The focal point could be a shoe bag or marking on the track about 10 to 15 feet back from the circle. As athletes initiate the backward movement, they should keep their eyes on the focal point until they have landed in the power position.

Spin   The spin is the other technique for building up momentum by moving across the ring. Many people consider the spin to be an advanced technique, and indeed it is. However, most of the top male shot-putters rotate, and some of your athletes may want to try it (elite women, by the way, are less likely to use the spin style). With some practice, even young children can develop proficiency in the fundamentals of the spin.

The power position used with the spin is essentially the same as in the glide style, but the footwork is different. The footwork for the spin technique is actually the same pattern as for the discus throw. The athlete lines up in the back of the ring with his back to the direction of the throw (see figure 10.11*a*). For right-handed throwers, the first movement is a shift onto the left foot and a forward three-quarter rotation (see figure 10.11*b*). The right foot comes down in the middle of the ring, and the left leg moves behind the right during a backward half rotation (see figure 10.11*c*). This spin puts the athlete into the power position. (For more detail about the footwork of the spin style, refer to the discus section later in this chapter.)

You need to be aware of certain safety issues when athletes use the spin technique for putting the shot. First, with the spin technique, there is a greater possibility that an athlete will miss the designated landing area. Take this into consideration and keep the area clear. Second, rotation can cause the shot to pull away from the body because of *centrifugal force*. This can also be a safety concern. Athletes need to be instructed to keep the shot against their neck by maintaining firm pressure. Third, you must make sure that your athletes keep the nonthrowing arm long and held out from the shoulder for balance. Although this is also true when throwing the discus, it is even more important in the shot put, especially for children as they are developing strength.

a   b   c

Figure 10.11   Moving across the ring using the spin.

Shot Put Activities

The putting movement is not as natural as the overhand throwing motion. Therefore, you will need to be patient and provide many different learning and training experiences to prepare children for competition. Training needs to include drills that help athletes learn the technique as well as drills and activities that help them gain the specific balance and strength needed to be successful.

GROUND RELEASES

Athletes begin by standing with the feet slightly wider than shoulder-width apart. They should be standing on a surface that will not be damaged by the shot, such as the shot put pit or a grassy area (note that athletes should never throw the shot on grass sport fields because it will leave indentations that could cause injury). The shot is held in position pressed against the neck. The athletes bend at the knees and waist, rotate the trunk, and then push the shot into the ground between their feet. This drill helps athletes develop strength for the arm strike as well as proper release mechanics. It is a drill that many shot-putters will do long into their career. Advanced athletes can perform 6 to 10 repetitions as a warm-up for practice or competition. Beginners may do 2 or 3 sets of 10 throws as a drill to learn the movement and to develop specific strength.

TWO-STEP

Two-stepping across the ring can help athletes learn the feel of getting momentum before the power position. It also helps an athlete feel the power of torque because the landing in the power position sets up shoulder–hip separation. The athlete begins in the back of the circle in a position similar to the start of the glide technique, except the feet are reversed. For a right-handed shot-putter, the left foot will be firmly on the ground, and the right foot will be held up or just resting on the toes. To begin the move, the athlete unseats as in the glide technique for putting the shot. Again, unseating is like sitting down on the couch—however, there is no couch to land on in the shot put circle, so the legs have to shift under the body to support the controlled fall. In the case of the two-step drill, the right leg shoots back into the middle of the ring. The athlete should aim the right foot to land in the position it is normally in for throws from a standing power position. The left leg pushes against the throwing surface and whips low and fast in front of the body to land in the front of the circle. This landing position is the power position stance. When both feet land, the shot-putter lifts, rotates, blocks, and strikes.

STANDING THROWS

Standing throws are a staple of the training program for shot-putters. This activity involves simply performing the throw from the power position. Athletes must be sure to make high-quality efforts—that is, although the drill may seem easy, the athletes must not develop bad habits by repeating mistakes. A coach should be present during the activity, and the athlete should work on staying focused and performing the move correctly. When an athlete's focus or technique deteriorates, it is time to end the activity.

MEDICINE BALL PUTS

In this activity, athletes perform a standing throw from the power position using a medicine ball. Smaller children and beginners should use 2- to 6-pound medicine balls. Intermediate and advanced children can work up to using 12-pound medicine balls.

The grip will be slightly different because the athlete uses two hands to control the ball. With a little practice, most children can learn to favor the throwing arm and simulate the proper arm strike while using the opposite hand just to stabilize. Because the ball is awkward to handle, it will be difficult for the athlete to throw with high intensity. Therefore, you should apply the concepts of range throwing and progressive loading (discussed previously). Less intensity means that more training volume is possible. Advanced athletes could work up to 50 medicine ball puts as the high end of progressive loading. For small children, keep the high end of a loading cycle at about 30 so they do not get bored.

Medicine ball puts with partners can help the athletes feel the rotational potential of the trunk. This drill works best with three children working together. One will be the putter, one the partner, and one the retriever. The putter and the partner face each other about 5 to 7 feet apart. The putter gets into the heel–toe stance with the partner in line with the direction of the throw. The retriever stands 30 to 50 feet behind the partner. The partner gently tosses the medicine ball at the putter's throwing shoulder. The putter catches with two hands, twists down into the loaded power position, and then lifts, rotates, and puts the medicine ball over the partner's head toward the retriever. This drill is slightly more intensive, so 2 or 3 sets of 5 to 10 throws per athlete is enough volume.

Discus

The discus is a weight that is shaped like a flying saucer. Athletes throw the discus using a sidearm slinging action. Great discus throwers speak of "flying" the implement rather than throwing it, which hints at the aerodynamic nature of the event. Most children quickly learn to execute a simple spin to build up momentum before the release. Because the discus flies farther than the shot put—and because the athletes rotate during the throw—a larger impact area and a protective cage are necessary. See figure 10.12 for an example of the cage layout for the discus.

The discus raises unique safety concerns. Essentially, the shape of the discus causes it to act like an airfoil or wing, slicing into the air at a specific angle. The discus is designed to ride the wind, so the flight pattern of the discus is not a true parabolic curve. If the discus catches the air, this might alter its course significantly, and when it lands, the discus can skid and hop in unpredictable directions. Because of this, nobody should be allowed in the impact area except for when retrieving the implements. It is wise to use an "everybody throws, everybody goes" method of retrieval—that means the children wait behind the cage while their teammates throw. When all the implements have been thrown, the ring is closed and all the athletes go and retrieve. Additionally, having two to four implements per person helps make practices go faster.

Another safety concern is related to the rotation used by discus throwers. As children are spinning with the discus, they sometimes get disoriented and throw significantly off target. A legal cage will contain the most errant throws. No one is allowed in the cage except for the thrower. Officials, coaches, and other throwers need to stay back 10 feet from the cage and stay away from the opening.

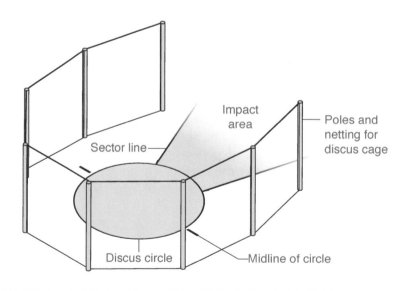

Figure 10.12   Discus cage and impact area.

Discus Technique

Discus technique can be broken down into these parts: grip, power position, and release. In addition, once athletes have mastered the discus technique discussed here, they can begin to learn the footwork and body positioning for the full spin (see "Full Spin" for more information).

Grip

The implement is held in a very loose grip with only the last digits of the fingers wrapping over the edge of the implement (see figure 10.13). Teach your athletes to allow the discus to stay balanced in their fingers through centrifugal force rather than by clutching the rim. One way of learning this is by doing walking turns. Athletes simply hold the discus with a proper grip and begin marching their feet up and down as they move in a circle on the spot. Centrifugal force will bring the arm up and press the discus into the fingers without the athlete having to grip the lip of the implement. Once your athletes have learned how to control the implement, they can begin to learn the throwing motion and the release for the discus.

Figure 10.13   Proper grip for the discus.

Power Position

To throw the discus from the power position, the athlete starts in a position that is similar to when putting the shot (as described previously). The feet are shoulder-width apart and aligned heel-toe with the direction of the throw; the knees and hips are slightly bent (see figure 10.14a). The athlete begins by holding the discus with two hands in front of the body. As the thrower begins the windup, body weight is shifted back away from the direction of the throw, and the athlete rotates the back toward the middle of the impact area (see figure 10.14b). As the implement moves back, the nonthrowing arm lets go of the implement and extends out for balance. The throwing arm swings the discus up and around the back of the body. Athletes should wind up to a point where they are still in balance.

The throwing motion starts with the lower body. The rotational and then lifting movements of the legs and hips begin the throwing motion. The nonthrowing side braces aggressively from the sole of the foot to the shoulder. The muscles of the chest, arm, and hand are fired last, whipping the throwing side of the body around.

Athletes must use the legs and hips to generate most of the initial movement. The arm should be very loose and whip around the body in the final stages

a

b

Figure 10.14   Power position for the discus.

Figure 10.15   Releasing the discus.

of summate force development. Trying to throw the discus with the arm is a common error. The arm and hand should guide the implement into its flight path and impart the final spin. It is easier to establish torque in the discus than in the shot put. It is also easier to lose torque. This is because of the length of the lever created by holding the implement at an arm's length away from the body. To help address this, you can use the coaching cue "Keep the discus high and back."

Release

Learning the proper release of the discus is crucial for success, so your athletes should spend a significant amount of practice time mastering the release. If the discus is released incorrectly, the aerodynamics will not work, and the implement will fall to the ground quickly. To get the discus to fly, an athlete must release it out of the front of the hand, and the index finger must impart spin on the discus (see figure 10.15). The release should involve an aggressive follow-through that includes flicking the hand to get the implement spinning.

Generally, the discus is released at about 33 to 38 degrees. This number represents the angle between the ground and the initial flight path of the center of mass of the discus. Another number to be aware of is the *angle of attack*. This is a measure of the angle between the surface of the discus and the angle of release. For children, a good starting point is to have these two measurements as close together as possible. Advanced throwers may adjust these angles to help fly the discus in changing wind conditions.

Full Spin

After an athlete masters the fundamentals of the power position throw, he or she can begin learning the full throw, also known as the full spin.

For the full spin, the athlete begins in the back of the circle with the feet slightly wider than shoulder-width apart. The athlete's feet should straddle the midline of the ring and the athlete's back should face the direction of the throw. After a windup toward the right, the athlete shifts his or her weight on the ball of left foot and executes approximately three-quarters of a full rotation, landing the right foot in the middle of the ring after a subtle flight phase. The left foot then rotates behind the right foot and lands in the power position. As a coach, you can use the turns and partial throws described in the next section to help your athletes develop the ability to turn and throw the discus.

Discus Activities

Discus throwing is a type of move that has to be learned, so you will need to be patient as you teach your athletes the essential technique for the event. To help athletes build a base of fundamental skill, you should use lots of drills and activities that involve technique development. Children have a good chance of being successful in this event if they are willing to put in the time it takes to learn the technique.

BOWLING AND FLIPS

Athletes stand 15 to 20 feet apart and use a bowling action to roll the discus back and forth to each other. They should not roll the discus aggressively or try to go for distance. The idea is to get the implement to roll straight at the partner. After athletes have some success in getting the discus to spin off the index finger and travel in a straight line, they can try the next step, which is flipping. Standing on the grass or dirt impact area, the throwers use the proper grip to hold the discus, but they hold it at the hip instead of at the side. The move can begin with some gentle swings to build up rhythm. The athlete flips the discus straight up in the air, working on the release off the index finger and trying to keep the discus vertical. Athletes should begin with flips that are only 1 to 3 feet in the air. Once athletes have control and consistency, they can try to flip slightly higher, perhaps 5 to 6 feet. Flipping the discus higher than 10 feet is not necessary and can be dangerous. The athletes should let higher throws drop to the ground rather than catching the discus.

Short flips for accuracy are the next step toward throwing from the power position. One way to do this drill is to have athletes spread out along the goal line of the football field. The flipping motion can be slightly higher than the hip, but the arm is not held out at the side of the body as in the power position throw. The athlete should hold the arm slightly above the hip at about 45 degrees. Again, a few swings can be used to build rhythm, and then the athlete flips the discus, aiming at the line 5 or 10 yards ahead. Everyone in the group goes at the same time. After everyone throws, the whole group walks forward, retrieves, lines up on the 10-yard line, and repeats the sequence. The drill continues up the field for a total of 10 throws. An appropriate goal is for athletes to develop consistency at doing two sets (down and back).

NONAERODYNAMIC STANDING THROWS

Standing throws using nonaerodynamic implements allow young athletes to concentrate on using the hips and legs, rotating the trunk, and whipping the arm to create a summate force. For this drill, you can use traffic cones. The athlete grips the pylon by the top, winds back, and throws. The length of the cone adds extra resistance and helps develop a smooth rhythm toward the summation of forces. You can also use hula hoops for this drill. More advanced athletes may use small weighted balls that are commonly used for javelin training.

TURNS

Following are specific turning activities that help athletes learn to rotate or spin on the ball of one foot:

- *Degree turns.* Many children are familiar with measuring rotations using the degrees of a circle because of skateboarding. A 180 is a half rotation, and a 360 is a full rotation. The athlete begins in a good athletic posture, with the feet shoulder-width apart. The arms are held wide. A discus can be taped or strapped to the throwing hand, or the athlete can hold a small weight. The drill can also be done with no implement. The athlete begins by rotating slightly in the opposite direction of the turn; the athlete then shifts the weight onto the turning foot and rotates to the intended position: a half, three-quarter, or full turn. These drills can also be done with backward rotations. Note that with forward rotations, the knees are held at least a foot apart (bowlegged), but in backward rotations, the legs can be closer together. This simulates the motion of the actual throw.

- *Skip turns on a line.* Forward and backward rotations can be put together into a sequence of turns performed while skipping. Right-handed throwers would begin with the left shoulder facing the direction of travel. The athlete starts with a forward 180-degree rotation on the left foot (with wide legs). This is followed immediately with a backward 180-degree rotation on the right foot (with tight legs). When the left foot touches down after the backward rotation, the athlete is in a position similar to the power position. At this point, the athlete can imitate a throwing action and then quickly settle back on the right foot and begin again—this series of actions resembles a skip. Three or four forward and backward combinations in a row demonstrates good balance and turning ability.

PARTIAL THROWS

For partial throws—commonly called "South African" throws in the track and field arena—the athlete starts with the left foot positioned in the back of the ring as if preparing to execute a full throw. The right foot, however, is positioned outside the ring and is already rotated 90 degrees in the direction of the throw. The athlete winds up, shifts the body weight onto the left leg, and does a forward 180-degree rotation into the middle of the ring. The athlete then rotates backward 180 degrees into the power position and initiates the hip and leg drive, the rotation of the trunk, and the final arm strike and release.

Note that for youth athletes, you have to be careful that they do not get "hooked" on the partial throw, because the rules for the discus state that both feet must be in the circle to begin the throw. Starting with the right foot outside of the ring adds to the potential for developing linear velocity. In addition, removing 90 degrees, rotating on the left foot, makes it easier to maintain balance. Younger and smaller children might be able to compete with some form of partial throw as they could fit the smaller turns in the circle. By late adolescence, however, young adults need to learn the full throw.

Javelin

The javelin throw is contested in the USATF Junior Olympics program. Athletes who are successful in this event come from many different backgrounds and come in all shapes and sizes. One thing that all successful javelin throwers have in common is shoulder flexibility. A good range of motion in the shoulder can be a predictor of the potential for success in this event. Speed and coordination are also attributes of top throwers.

The implement is shaped like a spear and is thrown overhead with one hand as in the softball throw. The vast majority of athletes use a run-up approach to build momentum before executing the throwing action in front of a painted foul line. The approach lane can have a synthetic track surface, or in some cases, the javelin is thrown off grass. Fair throws land tip first within a 34.92-degree sector. See figure 10.16 for an example of the javelin area.

During javelin training and competition, close attention must be paid to safety. Being in the path of a flying spear is obviously extremely dangerous. However, this is not the only way to get hurt. People standing behind throwers can also be struck by the tail end of the javelin if they are not careful. And the javelin does not always stick in the ground on landing. Sometimes the javelin bounces or skids, and either end can cause damage to those nearby. For more information on safety, see "Throwing Event Safety" earlier in this chapter on page 145.

Javelin Technique

The overhand motion used for throwing the javelin shares some similarities with the motion used for the softball throw. However, there are some important differences. The javelin is long and aerodynamic. Therefore, as in discus throwing, the angle of attack and the angle of release have to be considered. Beginners must practice lining up the javelin with the angle of release, which should be about 27 to 35 degrees. A common mistake is having the javelin too steep at release, causing the implement to have to push through the air. A coaching cue that you can use to help teach proper attack angle is "Throw through the point." Another major difference between the softball throw and the javelin throw is the follow-through. In the follow-through for the javelin, the throwing arm should not cross the midline of the body. Crossing over is common in ball throwing, but it may impart a twist on the javelin that will impede its aerodynamic efficiency. The proper follow-through is demonstrated by rotating the thumb down and whipping the arm down to the same side of the body.

To begin, the athlete grips the javelin with one or more fingers behind the cord. The palm faces up throughout the run-up and the throw. Three grip styles are common: American, Finnish, and forked. For the American grip, the index finger and the thumb push against the cord (see figure 10.17a). For the Finnish grip, the middle finger and the thumb push against the cord (see figure

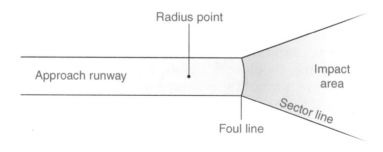

Figure 10.16   Javelin area.

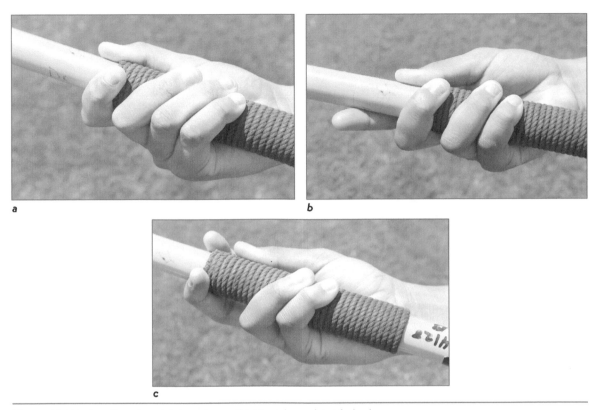

Figure 10.17   Javelin grips: *(a)* American, *(b)* Finnish, and *(c)* forked.

10.17*b*). In the forked grip, the thumb wraps around the top of the cord, and the index finger and middle finger push against the cord (see figure 10.17*c*).

A run-up is used to help build momentum and start the summate force development. The run-up should be smooth and rhythmic, with only as much speed as the athlete can handle. At the beginning of the approach, the implement is held near the ear and parallel with the ground (see figure 10.18*a*). About 15 to 20 feet from the foul line, the athlete withdraws the implement back into the throwing position (see figure 10.18*b*). Running with the spear back initiates what are called *cross steps*.

A major misconception in track and field is that the cross steps in the javelin include a step that goes behind the other leg. This is not the case. The cross steps are left, right, left, right steps as in all running and walking, but the cadence is different to allow the left leg to land immediately after the right leg lands (see figure 10.19, *a-c*). Three cross steps are common, although some athletes use more. As the blocking leg hits on the final cross step, the throwing action begins. Athletes should leave enough space from the foul line for a large follow-through step—at least 5 feet and maybe more for faster or bigger throwers. Remember, at the end of the run, the athlete will plant the leg of the nonthrowing side for the block and come to almost a complete stop.

Figure 10.18   Javelin carry and withdrawal.

The key to the throwing action is to be aggressive with the hips while being patient with the arm. This causes a big stretch and helps develop torque. The athlete must brace the left side firmly and allow the throwing side to whip around.

Javelin Activities

The javelin throw puts incredible demand on the smaller muscles of the elbow and shoulder. Therefore, the training plan for javelin throwers should include a wide variety of activities, with full throws being only a small part of the program. This is important throughout the developmental span. Athletes will gain tolerance for more high-intensity throws with experience. However, at no point do athletes outgrow the need to work on shoulder and elbow stabilization.

Figure 10.19 Cross steps for the javelin.

BALL THROWS

Throwing a nonaerodynamic implement can help javelin throwers work on footwork and the development of the hips and trunk without worrying about perfecting the flight. That being said, the coach and the athlete should work together to watch for javelin-specific technique, especially making sure that the palm is facing up and the throwing arm is not crossing the midline of the body in the follow-through. Note that it may be difficult for small children to differentiate between the technique for throwing a ball and that for throwing a javelin. To help them make the distinction, have them try two-hand overhead throwing with a very light one- or two-pound medicine ball. The two-hand throw puts the throwing hand in a position that simulates the javelin release (thumb down, arm not crossing the midline).

STICKS ON THE FIELD

This is a classic drill that is done by all javelin throwers. The drill involves simply walking the length of the field and performing a series of short, controlled, technical throws. It is helpful for athletes to aim at a point on the ground no farther than 20 feet away. During this drill, the coach can help the athlete with details of the release mechanics.

CROSSES

Developing the rhythm, technique, and balance necessary for effective cross steps takes time. Javelin throwers should start working on this drill early in their career and continue throughout. Practicing the cross steps—with and without the javelin—is an important part of the training program. The cross steps have a similar cadence to a gallop. The right leg whips aggressively forward and up, causing a flight phase and allowing the left leg to come forward. This causes the left leg to land immediately after the right leg. In the final cross step, the left leg becomes the block. Athletes should work on keeping the throwing arm up and back and keeping the nonthrowing arm held up and in front for balance. For this drill, 8 to 10 cross steps can be done consecutively. For an intermediate thrower, 10 to 15 repetitions of 10 crosses would be a significant part of a workout. Cross steps can also be done with some resistance. For an extra challenge, have athletes pull a sled or a small tire while holding the rope like a javelin.

Hammer Throw

The hammer throw is part of the Junior Olympics program starting with the intermediate groups. This event is also contested at some high school meets. The implement used in the hammer throw consists of a heavy ball attached

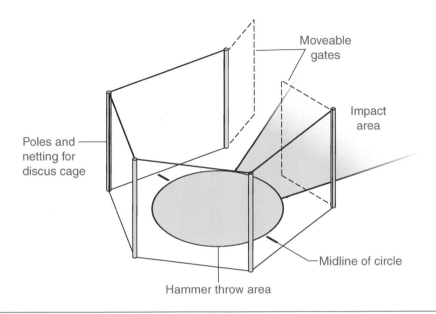

Figure 10.20   Hammer throw cage and impact area.

with a wire to a triangular handle. The ball is the size and weight of a shot, and the wire is over 3 feet long. Athletes use a rotational technique to throw the ball. Because athletes spinning around with heavy weights obviously poses some safety risks, the event must be practiced and contested from a large protective cage (see figure 10.20). Some, but not all, discus cages are large enough to use for the hammer throw. Also, the hammers cause significant damage to the fields they land on; therefore, the impact area should be designated as a hammer-only zone.

Hammer Throw Technique

The hammer is gripped using an overlapping technique. Right-handed throwers grip the handle with their left hand and cover their left with their right.

To get the ball moving, athletes use three or four preliminary swings, or winds above the head. The ball is placed on the ground to the right of the athlete (see figure 10.21a). Using the hands and arms, the athlete moves the handle to the left to cause the ball to start swinging (see figure 10.21b). As the ball begins to go behind the thrower, the arms bend and the hands move above and behind the head to guide the ball (see figure 10.21c). As the ball returns to the right side, the arms straighten and another swing can begin (see figure 10.21d). To build momentum, each swing can be slightly faster than the previous one.

After the swings, the athlete begins turning with the hammer. During the winds, the ball went around the athlete. During the turns, the thrower "locks

Figure 10.21   Preliminary swings for the hammer throw.

out" the hammer in front of the body and holds that position until the release. The athlete and the hammer rotate together around an axis roughly parallel to the spine. The footwork for the turns consists of double- and single-support phases. At the end of the last swing, the athlete is in double support and swings the ball to the left side. When the ball moves about 90 degrees from the starting point, the right foot is lifted up, and the athlete rotates on the left heel (see figure 10.22a). This is the beginning of the single-support phase. When the ball gets to 270 degrees, the right foot comes down, and the

a   b

Figure 10.22   Turns for the hammer throw.

athlete rotates on the balls of both feet back to 90 degrees again (see figure 10.22b). During this double-support phase, the athlete can accelerate the hammer by swinging toward the left side. Beginners often use only one turn. Advanced throwers use three or four turns.

The athlete releases the hammer when the ball is at 90 degrees. Instead of lifting the right foot and going into another turn, the athlete leaves both feet on the ground and aggressively lifts the arms up, delivering the hammer toward the impact area (see figure 10.23). Because the ball is rotating about an axis on a long wire, the ball will fly away on a tangent when it is freed from the axis. So, accurately throwing down the middle of the sector depends on releasing at 90 degrees.

Figure 10.23   Releasing the hammer.

Hammer Throw Activities

The hammer throw is a novel task for all children learning the event. You may find that many of your athletes have never even seen the event. Because of this, they will have a lot to learn about the technique, and they will need to develop a great deal of specific strength and balance. Following are some training activities that can be used to teach the hammer throw.

TURNS WITHOUT RELEASES

Hammer throwers must learn how to turn. These athletes should invest a great deal of practice time just practicing the turns without using releases. Athletes should be able to do six or seven turns without losing balance. Have the athletes start by holding a broom in front to simulate the hammer. As athletes advance, they can begin to practice turns using the real hammer.

RELEASES WITH MEDICINE BALLS OR SHOTS

This drill helps athletes learn how to release at the right time and deliver the hammer in the right direction. Place a cone 30 to 40 feet away from the thrower. This cone will be used as a target. The athlete begins by standing with the back toward the target. The athlete is gripping the medicine ball with both arms and holding it out over the right shoulder. Using the arms, the athlete swings the ball toward the left. When the arms are facing 90 degrees away from the starting position, the athlete lifts and delivers the ball. Doing 2 or 3 sets of 10 throws every other day for a month can be an essential step in learning the hammer throw. Advanced athletes can use the drill in a gym on rainy days.

MULTISWINGS

To gain the specific strength needed to execute the preliminary swings in the hammer throw, athletes should practice a number of swing variations. Athletes can swing the hammer using only the left or the right arm, or they can try to swing really slow and really fast. They can practice swinging using light hammers and heavy hammers. Athletes can also do wind variations while balancing on one foot, or they can send the ball around the body in the opposite direction. For an advanced athlete, 10 sets of 10 various swings (for a total of 100) would be a challenging drill. Beginners could do 10 sets of 5 swings.

11

Coaching Combined Events and Cross Country

I n this chapter, we cover two competitive opportunities related to track and field—combined events and cross country. Combined events are contested in the Junior Olympics program and include competitions such as the decathlon and heptathlon where athletes compete in multiple events with the goal of accumulating the most points for all those events. As mentioned, this chapter also includes information about the sport of cross country.

Combined Events

Combined-event competition is often considered to be the best measure of overall athletic ability. In the Junior Olympics program, combined-event competition is an outstanding opportunity for children with broad athletic ability to maximize their potential. With dedication and solid preparation, a good overall athlete with speed and jumping ability could have great success in the combined events. Often, athletes who are able to do most events pretty well fare better than athletes who are great at only one event.

The adult models of these events are the decathlon (10 events) for men and the heptathlon (7 events) for women. Developmentally appropriate options are used for youth athletes (as listed in table 11.1). For advanced athletes, the competition typically runs for two complete days, whereas younger children compete in modified combined-event competition with all of the events on the same day. For combined-event competition, one event is contested after another with brief breaks. The result of each event is tabulated into a score based on a standardized table. The athlete with the most points at the end is the winner.

See table 11.1 for a list of the combined events for each age group for the USATF Junior Olympics.

Combined-Event Competition

Combined-event competition often occurs as a separate meet from the other events, meaning that the only contests going on at the track at this time will be the combined events. Other times, especially at championships, the combined events are built into the schedule of a larger track meet. If this is the case, the results of the combined-event competition do not transfer to the open events. For example, if a heptathlete produces a high jump of 5 feet in the combined event, that result will not place in the open high jump. However, this athlete (if she is quite advanced) may compete in the open competition while also competing in the combined event. In all cases, the entrants in the combined events stay together as a group and move from one event to the next. Because of this, it is common to see a great deal of friendship and camaraderie develop among athletes and their support groups of parents and coaches, especially at the youth level.

Table 11.1 USATF Junior Olympics Combined Events

Bantam (ages 10 and under)	Triathlon	
	Shot put High jump 200-meter dash (girls); 400-meter dash (boys)	
Midget (ages 11 and 12)	Outdoor pentathlon	
	80-meter dash Shot put High jump Long jump 800-meter run (girls); 1,500-meter run (boys)	
Youth (ages 13 and 14)	Outdoor pentathlon	
	100-meter dash Shot put High jump Long jump 800-meter run (girls); 1,500-meter run (boys)	
Intermediate (ages 15 and 16)	Decathlon (boys)	
	Day one 100-meter dash Long jump Shot put High jump 400-meter dash	*Day two* 110-meter hurdles Discus throw Pole vault Javelin throw 1,500-meter run
	Heptathlon (girls)	
	Day one 100-meter dash High jump Shot put 200-meter dash	*Day two* Long jump Javelin throw 800-meter run
Young (ages 17 and 18)	Decathlon (young men)	
	Day one 100-meter dash Long jump Shot put High jump 400-meter dash	*Day two* 110-meter hurdles Discus throw Pole vault Javelin throw 1,500-meter run
	Heptathlon (young women)	
	Day one 100-meter dash High jump Shot put 200-meter dash	*Day two* Long jump Javelin throw 800-meter run

For combined events, an established order of events begins at a predetermined time with at least 30 minutes of rest between events. The games committees at each specific event may make minor alterations in the schedule to accommodate weather or conflicts with other events. Here are some basic rules that are used for combined-event competition:

- Athletes must make an attempt to start each event. Failure to do so will remove the athlete from the competition, and no final score will be given.
- Two false starts will disqualify a participant from a running event.
- Vertical jump progressions are as follows: For the high jump, the bar is raised in increments of 3 centimeters. For the pole vault, the bar is raised in increments of 10 centimeters.
- Athletes are allowed three attempts in the long jump and the throws.
- Long throws (discus and javelin) are measured to the least even centimeter.
- For other field events, measurements are to the least whole centimeter (no fractions of centimeters).

Preparing for Competition

Combined-event competition is usually an all-day commitment, so preparation is critical. Failure to prepare can lead to poor performance. As a coach, you can approach preparation from three perspectives: training, what to bring, and psychology.

Combined-Event Training

The guidelines for training for the combined events are similar to the ideas suggested for sprinters, jumpers, and throwers. Because the vast majority of events require explosive power, most of the training time is typically spent on the speed and strength events. In addition, the explosive events are very technical (hurdles, javelin throw, pole vault, and so on), and learning them takes time and practice.

Basic principles of training such as progressive loading, maximum velocity before speed endurance, and developmental considerations should be applied when athletes are training for the combined events. One unique aspect of combined-event training is that the athlete needs to prepare for the special kind of endurance it takes to compete for two days. Long practices would provide some experience in this regard; however, holding long training sessions for children is almost always a bad idea. As an alternative, you can have your athletes compete in several open events at big invitational track meets. This can help the athletes learn how to manage their energy, warm-up, hydration, and nutrition needs over a period of several hours.

A simple plan for organizing training for beginning athletes in the combined events is to practice the events as they fall into the standard two-day competition schedule. Practice all "day one" events one day, and then all "day two" events the next. In some cases, this pattern can be repeated twice before a rest day.

What to Bring

An athlete dashing to the car or the store in between events for a needed item wastes his or her valuable resting time. The best method of preparation is to tell your athletes to pack everything that they will need over the course of the competition. Here is a starter list:

- Uniforms
- Singlets (at least two)
- Bodysuit
- Underwear, compression tights, and so forth
- T-shirts and baggy shorts
- Sweat suit
- Rain gear
- Four or more pairs of socks (at least two for each day)
- Hat
- Sunglasses
- Sunscreen
- Extra shoelaces
- A few roles of athletic tape
- Spike kit
- Towels
- Chair and umbrella
- Music (be aware of rules regarding headsets)
- Books, toys, video games
- All necessary equipment
- Special equipment used for personal warm-ups (medicine balls, elastic bands, and so forth)

It is also a good idea to ask parents and volunteers to bring food and drinks for the day. Combined-event competitions at the youth level are usually small, and the concession stand, if there is one, will not likely be open. Further, the right kind of food for an athlete generally isn't available at a concession stand anyway. Competing all day is strenuous, and athletes need to be properly nourished. (Also see chapter 12 for more information on nutrition and hydration while competing.)

Psychology

As a coach, you need to be prepared for the mental demands of combined events and how they affect your athletes. It is particularly important to carefully monitor and control your athletes' arousal levels, ensuring that they are appropriate. Getting pumped for an event, then resting, and then getting pumped again can be very exhausting for young athletes, so take advantage of rest periods and teach your athletes how to relax during this time.

Another issue that tends to arise during combined events has to do with the natural highs and lows that come with competition. For example, there may be occasions when a few events go extremely well, causing an athlete to get overly confident, which creates problems for later events. There may also be occasions when an event early in the competition does not go well, requiring a special display of courage from the athlete in order to continue competing. Discuss these issues with your athletes and encourage them to think of a combined-event competition as one large, singular experience rather than numerous individual events. Personal bests and disappointments must both be taken in stride as an athlete focuses on maintaining consistency throughout the entire competition.

Cross Country

Cross country is a team sport that is closely related to track and field. In cross country, teams run courses set up on various types of terrain. The courses can range from one mile for the youngest children to five miles for advanced adolescents. Most distance runners—and some sprinters and jumpers—participate in cross country during the off-season.

While this extra training and competition can be good for young athletes, coaches and parents—and the athletes themselves—need to be very aware of the potential risks of overtraining and early specialization. Athletes that train all year for distance running can be at risk of shin splints and stress fractures. Additionally, it is important in the development of a young athlete that he or she be exposed to a wide range of movement experiences through early adolescence. Early specialization in cross country could potentially hinder general athletic development if the athlete is only focused on running. Therefore, it is generally in the athlete's best interest to be involved in other athletic endeavors in addition to cross country.

> **Coaching Tip**
>
> Be aware that true speed workouts will be compromised if the athletes are running on unstable surfaces. Athletes need to be prepared to run with unstable footing, but if pure leg speed is the goal of the workout, more stable surfaces such as the track or a sport field should be used.

Cross Country Competition

A strong team dynamic is essential for success in cross country. A group of five strong individual runners will often be beat in competition by a *team* of less talented runners who are highly united and competitive.

The specifics of scoring will depend on the organizing body and the developmental level. The typical system is that every runner who crosses the finish line is awarded points based on his finish. First place is awarded 1 point, second place gets 2 points, tenth place gets 10 points, and so on. Generally, the scores of the first five runners on a team are added together. The team with the lowest score wins the meet. Because the surfaces and terrain vary from course to course, times are less of a concern than placing.

In cross country, your athletes must learn that every point counts. Runners should battle for position all the way to the finish line. For every person who passes a fading runner, that is one more point for that runner's team, and one less point for the passing runner's team.

Cross Country Training

The basic principles of distance training outlined in chapter 8 apply to training for cross country runners. However, these athletes also need to work on skills that are specific to cross country.

The running surface for cross country is not consistent and uniform like a track. Not only does the running surface for cross country change from course to course, but each course might include a number of different surfaces. For example, a course might start and finish on grass soccer fields and may also include loops in wooded trails and some sections on gravel or paved road. You should help athletes prepare for this by providing training on the surfaces that athletes will encounter during competition, as discussed in the following sections.

Uphill and Downhill Running

While the track is flat, the cross country course will often have hills, and athletes need to be taught how to run up and down hills safely and effectively.

Running uphill greatly increases the strength demand and consequently puts more anaerobic stress on the athlete. Therefore, when designing training programs and tactics for cross country racing, you need to address two related and critical technical points: posture and overstriding. A common mistake is for athletes to bend at the waist and lean into the hill. This elongates the stride and puts pressure on the lower back and hamstrings. The upper body should stay upright relative to gravitational pull—that is, regardless of the angle of any incline, the spine should remain in a position that would be straight up and down on a flat surface. Because the forward foot will make contact with the ground earlier, stride length is reduced.

Running downhill can be fun for children, but it can also be dangerous. Running at uncontrollable speeds greatly increases the chances of tripping and causing serious injury. Also, running downhill with poor technique greatly increases the chance for injuries. While racing, runners might take risks in the heat of competition. You need to help cross country runners prepare for the inevitable downhills to reduce their chances of getting hurt.

As mentioned earlier in the book, the push-off in the running stroke causes a bit of a flight phase. Pushing off is not necessary when going downhill. As soon as the foot goes under the center of mass, it should be lifted and brought in front. Pushing off and causing flight while the ground is descending away will result in too much time in the air and long, dangerous strides. Again, the focus should be on high stride frequency and controlled stride length.

Some children will be able to get the "feeling" of what it means to not push off by imagining what it feels like to walk down stairs. As people descend stairs, their hips slightly lower as they position their base of support, avoiding the upward vertical forces that are typical in walking and running. In all cases, however, braking—that is, casting the lower leg too far in front of the body—should be avoided.

Repeats

Repeat timed efforts over a measured course are a staple of cross country training. Establish routes in your training area that are safe and easy to monitor. Create loops or out-and-backs that can be completed without having to stop or slow down for traffic. As much as possible, use routes that simulate the conditions of cross country courses. In training, athletes should run on hills and various surfaces that may be encountered during competition.

Race pace is often used during repeat workouts. Generally, it is a good idea to use a race pace that reflects an achievable goal for the end of the season rather than a pace that accommodates the runners' existing ability. This way runners can gain confidence in their ability to run faster over the course.

Ancillary Training

For cross country, athletes can use many types of training, besides just running, to prepare for the season.

For example, the locomotive moves described in the sprinting section on page 81 are important activities for cross country runners. These moves are effective for teaching the details about running style. Also, these exercises provide specific strength for the demands of running. Locomotive moves should be done on various surfaces and occasionally on hills. Athletes should be sure to do some lateral locomotive moves—such as sideways skips or carioca—because such a high percentage of activity for runners is straight ahead. This provides some strengthening of the support and stabilizing systems of the lower legs. Many coaches have their cross country runners do some locomotive moves every day. At a minimum, these exercises should be part of the program three days per week.

> **Coaching Tip**
> Any ancillary training activities can be done barefoot. Form running or doing locomotive moves with no shoes on provides a unique challenge and strengthens the foot. And, on late summer days it can be fun! Obviously, this should only be practiced in an area known to be free of broken glass or anything else that might damage runners' feet.

General strength circuits are also an important part of training for cross country runners. As young cross country athletes gain greater command of moving their own body weight, they will become more effective runners, and the ability to maintain posture during fatigue is an important attribute. This ability can be developed by implementing routines that include basic calisthenics for the trunk, hips, and upper body. Reinforce the team dynamic for cross country by having the athletes do circuits in unison led by members of the group.

Recovery

By using the many available resources to learn about workouts, most new coaches can soon feel relatively competent about putting together weekly, monthly, and season practice plans. Because there are so many different types of workouts, drills, and training activities, creating fun and interesting practices becomes easier as coaches begin to master their craft. Be cautious, however, because the very diversity of the training possibilities combined with coaches' and athletes' competitiveness can lead toward the slippery slope of overtraining. All athletes, especially distance runners, need rest time to regenerate and adapt to the training loads.

Most frequently, recovery happens by allowing days off from training. Typically, the athletes are instructed to stay relaxed during their day off and to not engage in vigorous activity in order to give their bodies a chance to recharge. Other times, the coach might want to have an organized practice to get the team together on a day when recovery is the goal of training. The following are some ideas for organized recovery sessions.

General Strength and Flexibility   After athletes are adapted to the initial stress of learning general strength and flexibility moves, these exercises can serve as a recovery workout if done in moderation. A 10- to 15-minute body weight circuit will facilitate greater circulation and help the regeneration process.

Recovery Runs   Running or jogging at a very comfortable pace can be a good activity for a recovery day. This is especially the case after a day of competition or hard workouts. Using running as recovery also helps increase the overall running volume of a training plan. Please note that recovery runs should not be the only type of recovery workouts. There are days when children should not run at all and should let their legs rest.

Instructional Sessions   Recovery days can be used to teach athletes about issues related to running. Young athletes should learn about goal setting, positive attitude, nutrition, and racing tactics. Spending time talking about these issues is a good investment and provides an opportunity for your athletes to grow as runners while letting the body rest and rejuvenate.

In addition, an instructional session could consist of getting together to watch a motivational movie. Several movies about running are available that would be inspiring and provide some instruction on the sport while allowing runners to lounge about and stay off their legs. Or, visual media could be used to learn about technique. The coach could videotape athletes at a hard workout or during competition and then use a recovery day to go over the film and teach about running style.

12

Coaching on Meet Day

Track meets provide the opportunity for your athletes to show what they've learned in practice. Just as your athletes' focus shifts on meet days from learning and practicing to competing, your focus shifts from teaching skills to coaching athletes as they perform those skills in competition. Of course, the track meet is a teaching opportunity as well, but the focus is on performing what has been learned, participating, and having fun.

In previous chapters, you learned how to teach your athletes skills; in this chapter, you will learn how to coach your athletes as they execute those skills in track meets. We provide important coaching principles that will guide you before, during, and after the competition.

Before the Meet

Many coaches focus on how they will coach only during the actual meet, when instead preparations should begin well before the first starting pistol blasts. Ideally, a day or two before a meet, you should cover several things—in addition to techniques and tactics—to prepare your athletes. Depending on the age group you are working with, you will need to create a specific plan for the upcoming meet based on information that is available to you. This will include making decisions on specific race tactics that you want your team to use. You should also discuss particulars such as what to eat before the meet, what to wear, what to bring, and when to be at the track.

Making Entries

Meet directors have different systems for managing entries. Systems vary depending on the meet, but they can be described in two broad categories: day-of-the-meet entries and advance entries.

Day-of-the-Meet Entries

At some all-comer meets, a very informal process is used for entries, simply requiring athletes to tell their name to the official so it can be written on a clipboard. When this is the case, coaches and parents need to make sure that athletes do not enter themselves in events they are not prepared for. The hurdles may look fun, but a meet is certainly not the place to learn how to run over them. At slightly more serious meets, coaches are required to sign up athletes on lists at a central registration table at the beginning of the meet. These lists are then distributed to event officials.

Advance Entries

For most invitational and all championship meets, entries are required in advance. Sometimes the coach is required to fill out a form listing the names, events, and entry marks for the team. Entry marks, sometimes called "seed marks" help the meet director put the athletes in the right heats and flights.

This mark should represent the anticipated performance at low key invitationals and must be a verifiable personal best at championship meets. The coach then faxes or mails the form to the meet director. Increasingly, meet directors are using online systems to handle entries. These systems require the coach to go online to a designated Web site and complete the entry process. Following are some general considerations regarding meet entries:

- Read all meet information carefully. For advance entries, there is always a deadline. Failure to meet the deadline could result in fines or may preclude the team from participation.

- Look over the schedule of events and think carefully about entries. Although an athlete may be very good at both the long jump and the javelin, these two events may be contested at the same time, and trying to do both would not work.

- Do not enter an athlete in several events in advance with the intention of waiting until meet day to choose which ones the athlete will do. This will cause empty lanes in the races and make the meet last longer. You should make the decision on which events an athlete will compete in before the entry deadline—and try to stick to that decision.

Communicating Entries

Make sure that athletes know which events they are entered in. Athletes should also be made aware of the schedule of events, the location of each event, and what time they are required to check in for their events. Some coaches make copies of the entries and hand them out to athletes and parents. For smaller groups, the coach may choose to simply tell the athletes what events they are entered in. In any case, communication is critical so that everyone knows what they are doing and where they are supposed to be.

When developing your plan, keep in mind that your athletes need to understand what you expect of them during the meet. Take time at the beginning or end of each practice to discuss these expectations. During the week before a meet, you should talk about race tactics and other issues related to the competition. Depending on the age level, experience, and knowledge of your athletes, you may want to let them help you determine race tactics and competition strategies. It is the coach's role to help youngsters grow through the sport experience. Allowing athlete input helps your children learn the sport and involves them at a planning level often reserved solely for the coach.

Coaching Tip

Many track clubs establish "base camps" at large invitational track meets. The coaches, parents, and athletes set up chairs and tents in one central area. The team uses this base camp as a meeting place and a spot to store bags and gear. The coach may want to set up a white board in this area in order to write key points such as "Check into events 30 minutes in advance" and "Drink water." The board can also be used as a place to post the entry list and the schedule.

It also gives them a feeling of ownership. Rather than just "carrying out orders" for the coach, they're executing the plan that they helped develop. Youngsters who have a say in how they approach a task often respond with more enthusiasm and motivation.

Discussing Premeet Details

Athletes need to know what to do before a meet, such as what they should eat on meet day and when, what clothing they should wear to the meet, what equipment they should bring, what time they should arrive, and what kind of warm-up they should do. You should discuss these particulars with them at the last practice before a meet. Here are some guidelines for discussing these issues.

Premeet Meal

In general, the goal for the premeet meal is to fuel the athlete for the upcoming competition and to provide energy for the brain. Some foods digest more quickly than others, such as carbohydrate and protein, so we suggest that athletes consume these rather than fat, which digests more slowly. Good carbohydrate foods include spaghetti, rice, and bran. Good protein foods include low-fat yogurt and skinless chicken. Athletes should eat foods that they are familiar with and that they know they can digest easily. Complete meals should be eaten three to four hours before the contest. Athletes who don't have time for a complete meal may use sport beverages and meal-replacement bars, but these shouldn't be used regularly as a replacement for the premeet meal.

The meet time will also affect the type of meal your athletes should consume. If the track meet starts right after school or early in the morning on the weekend, it won't be possible or practical for your athletes to eat three to four hours before the meet. In these situations, a lighter snack or breakfast will be more appropriate.

Coaching Tip

As discussed previously, you should have a preset plan or routine that is used before every meet. This can help alleviate nerves and build confidence in your athletes, especially those in younger age groups. A premeet routine will also help athletes forget outside concerns and get into the frame of mind to focus on competition.

Clothing and Equipment

Unless the team is traveling a long distance to compete, you should typically require that your athletes arrive in their team uniform, although they can put their spikes on at the track before the race. As discussed in chapter 3, the team uniform typically consists of shorts and matching singlets. Most meet organizers will supply starting blocks, but athletes are generally required to bring their own batons, throwing implements, and pole vault poles. Be sure to discuss equipment expectations at the preseason parent orientation meeting (as described in chapter 2).

Make sure that eyeglasses or sunglasses fit snugly on any athletes wearing them. If they don't, ask parents to provide their children with an elastic sport strap to hold the glasses in place. Athletes are allowed to wear braces or protective wraps to prevent injury or to protect current injuries, as long as the athletes are cleared by a doctor to participate. You should ask parents to ensure that their children are wearing required items when they come to the meet—you can't be responsible for the maintenance or fit of any such devices.

Arrival Time

You should instruct your athletes to arrive 30 to 40 minutes before meet time. All athletes need to adequately warm up before their events. Following are the suggested warm-up times for each age group:

- Ages 10 and under: 10 minutes before competition
- Ages 11 and 12: 20 minutes before competition
- Ages 13 and 14: 30 minutes before competition

Coaching Tip
Track and field meets are often all-day events. Therefore, you need to help athletes stay hydrated and fueled throughout the competition, not just before. For longer competitions, consider working with parents to rotate the responsibility for providing water or sports drinks, along with nutritious snacks such as fruit or crackers. See chapter 4 for guidelines on how much fluid your athletes should drink before, during, and after a contest.

Warm-Up

Athletes need to both physically and mentally prepare for a competition. Physical preparation involves warming up. We've suggested that athletes begin warming up 10 to 30 minutes before competition, depending on the age group. Younger athletes may begin warming up closer to the start time; this will help them stay focused and prevent them from getting too tired from the excitement of warming up and preparing to compete.

Warm-ups on meet day should be similar to warm-ups done at practice. You should let the athletes know where they are allowed to warm up on the track. Some facilities require warm-ups to be done on adjacent fields. The warm-up should consist of stretches, a few brief drills that focus on skill practice, and exercises that involve a range of motion (such as leg swings, trunk rotations, and arm circles).

You should refrain from delivering a long-winded pep talk, but you can help athletes mentally prepare for the competition by reminding them of the skills they've been working on in recent practices and by focusing their attention on their strengths and what they've been doing well. Also take time to remind athletes that they should support their teammates, compete hard and smart, and have fun!

Unplanned Events

Part of being prepared to coach is to expect the unexpected. What do you do if athletes are late? What if *you* have an emergency and can't make the meet or will be late? What if the meet is rained out or otherwise postponed? Being prepared to handle out-of-the-ordinary circumstances will help you when unplanned events happen.

If athletes are late, you may need to adjust your entries (if allowed). Although this may not be a major inconvenience, you should stress to your athletes that there are important reasons for being on time. First, part of being a member of a team is being committed to and responsible for the other members. When athletes don't show up, or show up late, they break that commitment. And second, athletes need to go through a warm-up to physically prepare for the competition. Skipping the warm-up increases the risk of injury.

There may be a time when an emergency causes you to be late or to miss a meet. In these cases, you should notify your assistant coach, if you have one, and the meet director. If notified in advance, a volunteer or a parent of an athlete might be able to step in for the meet.

Sometimes a meet will be postponed because of inclement weather or for other reasons such as unsafe track conditions. If the postponement takes place before meet day, you must call every member of your team to let them know. If it happens while the teams are on-site and preparing for the meet, gather your team members and explain why the meet has been postponed. Make sure all your athletes have a ride home before you leave—you should be the last to leave.

> **Coaching Tip**
> Although the site coordinator and meet director have the formal responsibilities for facilities, you should know what to look for to ensure that the environment is safe for all athletes (see "Facilities and Equipment Checklist" in appendix A on page 210). You should arrive at the track 45 to 60 minutes before meet time so you can check the facility, check in with the meet director and officials, and greet your athletes as they arrive.

During the Meet

Throughout the meet, you must keep the competition in proper perspective and help your athletes do the same. Observe how your athletes execute techniques, race plans, and tactics. These observations will help you decide on appropriate practice plans for the following week. Let's take a more detailed look at your responsibilities during a meet.

Tactical Decisions

You will need to make tactical decisions in several areas throughout a meet. You'll make decisions about who runs the relays, about opening heights in the

Communicating With Parents

The groundwork for your communication with parents will have been laid in the parent orientation meeting, where the parents learned the best ways to support their kids'—and the whole team's—efforts on the track. You should encourage parents to judge success based not just on the outcome of the events, but also on how the kids are improving their performances.

If parents yell at the kids for mistakes made during the meet, make disparaging remarks about the officials or opponents, or shout instructions on which techniques to focus on, you should ask them to refrain and to instead support the team through their comments and actions. These standards of conduct should all be covered in the preseason parent orientation meeting.

When time permits, as parents gather before a meet (and before the team has begun formal preparations for the competition), you can let them know in a general sense what the team has been focusing on during the past week and what your goals are for the meet. However, your athletes must come first during this time, so focus on your athletes during the premeet warm-up.

After a meet, quickly come together as a coaching staff and decide what to say to the team. Then, if the opportunity arises, you can informally assess with parents how the athletes did based not on the outcome but on meeting performance goals and competing to the best of their abilities. Help parents see the contest as a process, not solely as a test that is pass or fail, win or lose. Encourage parents to reinforce that concept at home.

For more information on communicating with parents, see page 18 in chapter 2.

vertical jumps, about making slight adjustments to your athletes' technique, and about dealing with athletes' performance errors.

Choosing Relay Teams

If your team is large and you have several talented runners, choosing four athletes to run the relay may be difficult. However, a more frequent problem is having only two or three fast kids and trying to find runners to fill open spots. If the latter is the case, make sure that you do not put someone in the relay who might be at risk of humiliation or injury. Putting an overweight thrower in the relay just to fill a spot is not a good idea. The overall team performance will likely suffer, and the child could get hurt and embarrassed. If you have five or more runners who deserve to be on the relay team, you will be required to make selections—much like a basketball coach choosing a starting lineup. When selecting runners for the relay, take the following into consideration: steadiness under pressure, ability to work as a team member, and ability to handle the baton.

Keeping a Proper Perspective

Winning is the short-term goal of your track and field program. The long-term goal is helping your athletes learn the techniques, tactics, and rules of track and field; how to become fit; and how to be good sports on the track and in life. Your young athletes are "winning" when they are becoming better human beings through their participation in track. Keep that perspective in mind when you coach. You have the privilege of setting the tone for how your team approaches the track meet. Keep winning and all aspects of the competition in proper perspective, and your young charges will likely follow suit.

In some cases, it might be better to have a slightly slower athlete who is always dependable, is a great team member, and has really good hand–eye coordination than a fast and unreliable runner.

Choosing Opening Heights in Vertical Jumps

The coach and athlete must work together to determine the best height for the jumper to enter the competition at. Generally, novice jumpers enter at the lowest height at the beginning of the competition. Advanced jumpers, however, might find it advantageous to pass on the low heights and wait for the bar to move up a few times before jumping. A variety of issues need to be considered when making this decision. If an athlete passes on too many heights, the time between warm-up and jumping in competition might be too long. In this case, the athlete may want to take a jump at a height that seems low in order to stay warmed up. Weather might also be a variable that must be taken into account. If it is cold and windy, attempting to enter the competition at an advanced height may be a mistake. In this situation, the jumper might do well to come in early and get in some safe jumps. On the other hand, if conditions are good and the athlete needs to clear an advanced height to qualify for a championship meet, the athlete should consider passing on the low heights. This will enable the jumper to have fresh legs to jump at the advanced heights.

Correcting Errors

In chapter 6, you learned about two types of errors: learning errors and performance errors. Learning errors occur because athletes don't know how to perform a skill. Performance errors are made not because athletes don't know how to execute the skill, but because they make mistakes in carrying out what they do know.

Sometimes it's not easy to tell which type of error athletes are making. Knowing your athletes' capabilities helps you determine if they know the skill and are simply making mistakes in executing it or if they don't know how to perform it. If they are making learning errors—that is, they don't know how to perform the skills—you should note this and cover it at the next practice. Competition is not usually the best time to teach skills.

> **Coaching Tip**
> Designate an area near the team's "base camp" where athletes report after competing. In this area, you can speak to them either individually or as a group and make necessary adjustments.

If they are making performance errors, however, you can help athletes correct those errors during a meet. Athletes who make performance errors often do so because they have a lapse in concentration or motivation, or they are simply demonstrating human error. Competition can also adversely affect a young athlete's technique, and a word of encouragement about concentration may help. If you do correct a performance error during a meet, do so in a quiet, controlled, and positive tone of voice between jumps or throws or when the athlete is sitting in the stands or at base camp with you.

For those making performance errors, you must determine if the error is just an occasional error that anyone can make or if it is an expected error for a youngster at that stage of development. If the latter is the case, then the athlete may appreciate your not commenting on the mistake. The athlete knows it was a mistake and may already know how to correct it. On the other hand, perhaps an encouraging word and a "coaching cue" (for example, "Be tall as you run your curve!") may be just what the athlete needs. Knowing the athletes and what to say is very much a part of the "art" of coaching.

Coach and Athlete Behavior

Another aspect of coaching on meet day is managing behavior—both yours and your athletes'. As a coach, it is your responsibility to control emotions when the track meet is not going the way that you or your athletes would have hoped.

Coach Conduct

You very much influence your athletes' behavior before, during, and after a meet. If you're up, your athletes are more likely to be up. If you're anxious, they'll take notice, and the anxiety can become contagious. If you're negative, they'll respond with worry. If you're positive, they'll compete with more enjoyment. If you're constantly yelling instructions or commenting on mistakes and errors, it will be difficult for athletes to concentrate. Instead, you should let athletes get into the flow of the competition.

The focus should be on positive competition and on having fun. A coach who overorganizes everything and dominates a meet from the side of the track is definitely not making the contest fun. So how should you conduct yourself? Here are a few pointers:

- Be calm, in control, and supportive of your athletes.

- Encourage athletes often, but instruct during competition sparingly. Athletes should focus on their performance during competition, not on instructions shouted from the bleachers.

- If you need to instruct an athlete, do so in an unobtrusive manner when you're standing near each other. Never yell at athletes for making a mistake. Instead, briefly demonstrate or remind them of the correct technique, and encourage them. Tell them how to correct the problem when it is their turn to compete again.

You should also discuss meet demeanor as a coaching staff, making sure everyone is in agreement regarding proper conduct on the track and at the base camp. Once these expectations are agreed on, stick with them. Remember, you're not competing for an Olympic gold medal! At this level, track meets are designed to help children develop their skills and themselves—and to have fun. So coach in a manner at meets that helps your athletes achieve these objectives.

Athlete Conduct

You're responsible for keeping your athletes under control. Do so by setting a good example and by disciplining when necessary. Set team rules for good behavior. If athletes attempt to cheat, fight, argue, badger others, yell disparaging remarks, and the like, it is your responsibility to correct the misbehavior. Initially, this may mean removing athletes immediately from the competition, letting them calm down, and then speaking to them quietly, explaining that their behavior is not acceptable for your team—and that if they want to compete, they must not repeat the action. You must remember, too, that younger athletes are still learning how to deal with their emotions in addition to learning the sport. As a coach, you must strive to remain calm during times when young athletes are having trouble controlling their emotions.

Consider having team rules in these areas of conduct:

- Athlete language
- Athlete behavior
- Interactions with officials
- Discipline for misbehavior
- Dress code for competitions

Athlete Welfare

All athletes are not the same. Some attach their self-worth to winning and losing. This idea is fueled by coaches, parents, peers, and society, which places great emphasis on winning. Athletes become anxious when they're uncertain whether they can meet the expectations of others—especially when meeting a particular expectation is important to them also.

If your athletes look uptight during a meet, you should find ways to reduce both the uncertainties about how their performance will be evaluated and the importance they are attaching to competition. Help athletes focus on realistic personal goals—goals that are reachable and measurable and that will help them improve their performance while having fun as they compete. Another way to reduce anxiety on meet day is to avoid emotional premeet pep talks. Instead, remind athletes of the techniques and strategies they will use, and urge them to compete hard, to do their best, and to have fun.

When coaching during meets, remember that the most important outcome of participating in track and field is building or enhancing athletes' self-worth. Keep that firmly in mind, and strive to promote this through every coaching decision.

Keeping the Meet Safe

Chapter 4 is devoted to safety, but it's worth noting here that safety during meets can be affected by how officials run the meet. If officials aren't keeping things organized and this risks injury to your athletes, you must intervene. Voice your concern in a respectful manner, and place the emphasis where it should be—on the athletes' safety. One of an official's main responsibilities is to provide for athletes' safety. Both you and the officials are working together to protect the athletes whenever possible. Don't hesitate to address an issue of safety with an official when the need arises.

Opponents and Officials

You must respect opponents and officials. Without them, there wouldn't be a competition. Opponents provide opportunities for your team to test itself, improve, and excel. Officials help provide a fair and safe experience for athletes and, as appropriate, help them learn the sport. Officials are usually volunteers.

You and your athletes should show respect for opponents and officials by giving your best efforts and being civil. Don't allow your athletes to "trash talk" or taunt a competitor or an official. Such behavior is disrespectful to the spirit of competition, and you should immediately remove an athlete from a meet (as discussed previously in "Athlete Conduct") if that athlete disobeys your team rules in this area.

Remember, too, that officials at this level are often parents—in many cases not specifically trained—and the level of officiating should be commensurate with the level of competition. In other words, don't expect perfection from officials any more than you do from your athletes. Especially at younger levels when the events are not chapionships, officials might be more liberal about foot fouls in the throws, for example, because if they weren't, many children would not get a mark. As long as the calls are being made consistently for all competitors, most of your officiating concerns will be alleviated.

After the Meet

When the meet is over, join your athletes in congratulating the coaches and athletes of the opposing teams, then be sure to thank the officials. Check on any injuries athletes sustained, and inform athletes about how to care for them. Be prepared to speak with the officials about any problems that occurred during the meet. Then, hold a brief team meeting to ensure that your athletes are on an even keel, whether they met their goals or not.

Reactions After a Meet

Your first concern after a meet should be your athletes' attitudes and mental well-being. You don't want them to be too high after a first-place finish or too low after a poor performance. This is the time you can be most influential in helping athletes keep the outcome in perspective and settle their emotions.

When your athletes are celebrating great performances, make sure they do so in a way that doesn't show disrespect for the other competitors. It's okay and appropriate to be happy and celebrate a great result, but don't allow your athletes to taunt the opponents or boast about their victory. If an athlete loses a close race, the athlete will naturally be disappointed. But, if your runner has made a winning effort, let the athlete know this. After a loss, help athletes keep their chins up and maintain a positive attitude that will carry over into the next practice and contest. Winning and losing are a part of life, not just a part of sport. If athletes can handle both equally well, they'll be successful in whatever they do.

Postmeet Team Meeting

After the meet, gather your team in a designated area for a short meeting. Before this meeting, decide as a coaching staff what to say and who will say it. Be sure the staff speaks with one voice after the meet.

If your athletes have performed well in a meet, you should compliment them and congratulate them. Tell them specifically what they did well, whether they won or lost. This will reinforce

Coaching Tip

Before conducting the postmeet team meeting, you should lead your athletes through a cool-down similar to the one you use to end your practice sessions. This will not only help athletes improve their flexibility, but it will also help them calm down after the meet so they can focus on what you are about to say. The younger the athletes, the shorter your postmeet cool-down and team meeting should be. For athletes who are 10 and under, keep the postmeet routine to no more than 10 minutes; for older athletes, keep it to no more than 15 minutes.

their desire to repeat their good performances. Don't use this time to criticize individual athletes for poor performances in front of teammates, and don't go over technical problems and adjustments, either. You should help athletes improve their skills, but do so at the next practice. Immediately after a meet, athletes won't absorb much technical information.

Finally, make sure your athletes have transportation home. Be the last one to leave in order to ensure full supervision of your athletes.

13

Developing Season
and Practice Plans

We hope you've learned a lot from this book: what your responsibilities are as a coach, how to communicate well and provide for safety, how to teach and shape skills, and how to coach during competitions. But competitions make up only a portion of your season—you and your athletes will spend more time in practices than in competition. How well you conduct practices and prepare your athletes for competition will greatly affect not only your athletes' enjoyment and success throughout the season, but also your own.

Fun Learning Environment

Regardless of what point you're at in your season, you should work to create an environment that welcomes learning and promotes long-term development. Following are seven tips to help you and your coaching staff get the most out of your practices:

1. Stick to the practice times agreed on as a staff.

2. Start each practice with an appropriate warm-up.

3. Keep the practice routine as consistent as possible so that the athletes can feel comfortable.

4. Be organized in your approach by moving quickly from one activity to another and from one stage of training to another.

5. Tell your athletes what the practice will include before the practice starts.

6. Allow the athletes to take water breaks whenever possible.

7. Focus on providing positive feedback.

Season Plans

Your season plan acts as a snapshot of the entire season. Before the first practice with your athletes, you must sit down as a coaching staff and develop such a plan. To do so, simply write down each practice and meet date on a calendar, and then go back and number the practices. These practice numbers are the foundation of your season plan. First, imagine the kind of fitness you would like your athletes to demonstrate at the end of the season. Also imagine the kind of training that the team will do during the final weeks leading up to the most important championship. Then, moving backward from practice to practice, outline a systematic progression that will lead to those fitness and training goals. Determine what you will cover in each practice and what kind of training will be done. You should note the purpose of the practice, the main skills you will cover, and the activities you will use.

In track and field, coaches generally use an approach to training called *periodization*. Periodization simply means that the year or season is divided into periods, each with a specific training goal. In the classic model, the year or season is broken into three periods: rest or off-season, preparation period, and competition period. The preparation and competition periods are then broken down further into two phases. The preparation period is divided into general and specific preparation, and the competition period is divided into early competitions and championships.

Ideally, the preparation period will be about half of the overall training for the year. This is not always practical because some track teams might have an early competition after only a few practices. Nevertheless, the spirit of the early practices should be very general, and the goal is to prepare the whole body for the more specific training to come. The idea is to get a higher volume of work in to build overall fitness. This means that the intensity must remain moderate or low. Here are some examples of general preparation activities:

- Throwing medicine balls
- Core stability work
- Skipping and rhythmic jumps on grass fields
- Barefoot running
- General strength moves and calisthenics
- Multistart drills
- Running over very low hurdles
- Balance and lower leg stability work
- Flexibility development (both static and dynamic)

As athletes begin to get into shape, preparation can become more specific to the events of track and field. This is when the coach begins to help athletes figure out the techniques of the various events and develop the movement patterns that are related to successful throwing, jumping, and running. Although the training begins to look more like what will happen in competition, the primary goal is still to improve fitness, with a secondary aim of learning technique. The overall volume remains high, and the intensity remains moderate. Here are some examples of specific preparation:

- Learning the block starts
- Hurdle mobility drills
- Fartlek runs
- Parlov relays

- Throwing drills
- Circle runs with a pop-up
- Relay exchange practice
- Runway rehearsals for the long jump and triple jump
- Pole vault drills

Coaching Tip

While developing your season plan, keep in mind that you will want to incorporate the games approach into your practices. The games approach focuses on replicating the competitive environment. When appropriate, using modified competitive activities better prepares the athletes, both physically and mentally, for the demands of competition. This can be as simple as making sure to time most full-speed efforts. A more elaborate setup would be to stage relay races that allow athletes to have a fun competition while learning baton-passing technique and getting in some aggressive running.

Early meets are the time athletes begin to put together the skills they will use in competition. It is okay for athletes to go to the first few meets with imperfect technique. The meets that matter most are at the end of the season. During the period of the early meets, intensity of training begins to increase, and consequently, volume must be decreased. The track meets (one or two per week) will be a major part of the overall training. Work is more focused on increasing intensity and mastering technique. Here are some of the things that happen during the early part of the competitive period:

- Time trials in practice
- Rehearsals of full technique in the field events
- High-intensity distance runs
- Competitions at track meets
- Range throwing

Finally, as the season nears completion, the championship meets arrive. In some cases, athletes might have three or four championship type meets. In other cases, there will only be one championship meet at the end of the season. During this period, it is too late to develop new levels of fitness, and the focus of training is perfecting technique and executing high-level efforts. Rest is critical at this point. Because athletes are used to more training volume, they may get a bit restless now that they have less work to do. The coach must encourage the athletes to use their extra energy when it counts—at a track meet. Activities during the championship phase include the following:

- Video analysis
- Planning sessions to address tactics and strategy
- Testing and measurement at practice

- Traveling to high-level competitions and competing for lifetime-best results
- High-intensity, low-volume training sessions with large rest intervals

Following is more detailed information about season plans for each particular age group—ages 8 to 9, ages 10 to 11, and ages 12 to 14.

Season Plan Considerations for Ages 8 to 9

Many children 8 years old and younger have had little or no exposure to track and field. Don't assume they have any knowledge of the sport. Help them explore the basic skills, such as throwing for distance, jumping for height or distance, and running against time and competitors. Keep practices playful throughout the entire season. Use many different training activities during each session. Try to design the activities so that children stay active and have plenty of opportunities to participate. Standing in line while waiting for a turn makes it difficult for children to stay engaged. Technique should be introduced in a fundamentally sound fashion. However, the natural style that children bring to running, jumping, and throwing is often perfectly acceptable. Although young children will go to meets and compete, the main focus should be on participation, learning the rules, and having fun.

Season Plan Considerations for Ages 10 to 11

Children in the 10- to 11-year age group can begin training with a bit more specificity. However, the coach should try to make sure that the practices are fun and that children are engaged. It is too early to make practices into serious workouts. Children can be challenged and begin some organized training, but a general and fun approach should be used. Development of postural strength must take place before a detailed approach to technique can be emphasized.

Season Plan Considerations for Ages 12 to 14

In this age group, athletes are refining the skills they have learned from past years. The season plan for this age group builds on those for the two previous age groups and adds more specific skills. Postural strength should be developed to the point where athletes can demonstrate some mastery of technique. Athletes can benefit from more intense and structured training. Competitions begin to get more serious, including advancement to national championships. Nevertheless, athletes at this age, though they may act grown up, are still very young. If training becomes too rigorous and serious, or competitions become too intense, athletes may begin to lose interest in the sport.

Developing Practice Plans

Coaches rarely believe they have enough time to practice everything they want to cover. To help organize your thoughts and help you stay on track toward your practice objectives, you should create practice plans. These plans help you better visualize and prepare so that you can run your practices effectively.

When developing daily practice plans, the first step is to consider how the flow of your practices will fit together over the course of one week. First, consider the limitations that may affect your plans: facility constraints, competitions, weather issues, and other commitments that the athletes or coaches may have. Many clubs only have access to tracks on certain days of the week. Furthermore, some coaches may only be able to help out on a couple of nights a week. Scheduling a hurdle workout on Tuesday may look good on paper, but if you have no access to a track and the hurdle coach has to work, the plan will not be practical. Carefully considering the limitations beforehand allows the coach to identify these conflicts. Once you have a clear understanding of the constraints, you can put together a weekly plan that works in your context by creating daily practice plans. The flow of the daily practice plans should be designed so that the practice sessions fit together in a way that is not only practical, but also maximizes the training effect. For example, a high-intensity and explosive workout that involves full-speed running and jumping exercises should be followed by a less explosive training session the next day. The day before a competition should be fairly low volume so that the athletes go into the meet with fresh legs. This will help them feel confident about their ability to do their best.

Remember that your daily practice plans should be age appropriate for the age group you are coaching. The plans should incorporate all of the skills and concepts presented in the particular age group's season plan. To begin, each practice plan should note the practice objective (which is drawn from your season plan) and the equipment necessary to execute the specific activities in the practice. Each practice plan should also include a warm-up and cool-down. During the cool-down, coaches should attend to any injuries suffered during practice and make sure that the athletes drink plenty of water.

Following are sample practice plans covering a week of practice for combined-event athletes in the 8- to 9-year age group. You can use these sample plans as a guide when developing plans for your team.

Monday

Objective
Develop explosive power and technique

Equipment
Watch, cones, shovel and rake, shot put

Training Units
- Warm-up—400-meter jog, skipping and running drills, loosening moves
- Acceleration work from a standing start—15 repetitions of a 10-meter explosive start (with walk back as recovery)
- Pop-ups into the long jump pit (10 repetitions)
- Shot put throws from a standing position (10 throws)
- Cool-down—400-meter jog and static stretching

Tuesday

Objective
Recovery and rhythm work

Equipment
Cones, six hurdles

Training Units
- Warm-up—fast walking (6 × 100 meters)
- Drills to work on running technique
- Rhythm running on grass (4 to 6 × 75 meters at 100-meter time)
- Hurdle mobility circuit
- Push-ups and sit-ups; general strength circuit
- Cool-down—static stretching

Wednesday

Objective
Strength and speed endurance

Equipment
Watch, cones, medicine balls, shovel and rake

Training Units
- Warm-up—400-meter jog, skipping and running drills, loosening moves
- Full long jump attempts practicing the style to be used at meets (6 attempts)
- Sprints (3 × 150 meters with a 250-meter walk around the track as recovery)
- Medicine ball throws (20 throws)
- Cool-down—easy jog and static stretching

Thursday

Objective
Recovery

Equipment
None

(continued)

Thursday, *continued*
Training Units
- Warm-up—easy jog on grass and loosening moves
- General strength circuit
- Discussion of meet plans while athletes perform static stretches

Friday
Competition

Saturday
Rest

Sunday
Encourage athletes to play outside for at least three hours (e.g., swim, bike, play in the yard).

Constructing practice plans requires both organization and flexibility on your part. Don't be intimidated by the amount of training that you want to cover. Pick out a few basics and build your initial practice plans around them; this process will get easier after you've drafted a few plans. Then you can move from teaching simple concepts and skills to drawing up plans that introduce more complex ones. Build in some flexibility—if you find that what you've planned for practice isn't working, you should have a backup activity that approaches the skill or concept from a different angle. The top priorities are to keep your athletes involved in practice and to help everyone have fun while they're learning.

Appendix A

Related Checklists and Forms

This appendix contains checklists and forms that will be useful in your track and field program. All checklists and forms mentioned in the text can be found here. You may reproduce and use these checklists and forms as needed for your track and field program.

Facilities and Equipment Checklist

Facilities

Track

- ❑ The running surface is free of debris.
- ❑ Equipment (benches, hurdles, brooms, rakes, and so on) is positioned properly to not cause a tripping hazard.
- ❑ Large puddles are swept free of standing water.
- ❑ The surface of the track is in good condition (free of holes or tears).
- ❑ Track markings are clear. Coaches, athletes, and meet officials understand what the markings mean.

Field event areas

- ❑ Sprinkler heads and openings are at grass level.
- ❑ The field is free of toxic substances (lime, fertilizer, and so on).
- ❑ The field is free of low spots or ruts.
- ❑ Impact areas for throws are free of other equipment and debris.
- ❑ No rocks or cement slabs are on the field.
- ❑ The field is free of protruding pipes, wires, and lines.
- ❑ Flags and signage are in place to section off areas for the throws.
- ❑ The field is not too wet.
- ❑ The field is not too dry.
- ❑ The sector lines are well marked.
- ❑ Jumping approach surfaces are clean and in good repair.
- ❑ Jumping takeoff boards are free of excessive wear and are well marked.
- ❑ Foam landing surfaces conform to current rules, are in good condition, and are properly assembled.
- ❑ Sand landing surfaces are free of debris, tilled to at least 10 inches, and raked.

Throwing areas

- ❑ The concrete circles are well marked with clear center marks and foul lines.
- ❑ The area is free of debris.

From ASEP, 2008, *Coaching youth track & field* (Champaign, IL: Human Kinetics).

❑ The protective cage and netting are in good condition (free of holes and properly installed).

❑ The areas for spectators are clearly marked and flagged.

❑ Brooms and towels are available to keep the area clean.

Equipment

Coach's bag

❑ Athletic tape

❑ Clipboards

❑ Extra water bottle

❑ Pens and pencils

❑ Safety pins

❑ Rain gear and umbrella

❑ Roster with emergency contact information

❑ Sidewalk chalk

❑ Small first aid kit

❑ Small permanent marker

❑ Spikes and spike wrench (if applicable)

❑ Sunscreen

❑ Tape measures

❑ Video camera

❑ Whistle

Parent's or athlete's bag

❑ Athletic tape

❑ Water bottle

❑ Nutrition bars

❑ Extra socks

❑ Spikes and spike wrench (if applicable)

❑ Sunscreen

❑ Extra T-shirt, shorts, and sweats

❑ Rain gear and umbrella

From ASEP, 2008, *Coaching youth track & field* (Champaign, IL: Human Kinetics).

Informed Consent Form

I hereby give my permission for _____ to participate in _____ during the athletic season beginning on _____. Further, I authorize the school or club to provide emergency treatment of any injury or illness my child may experience if qualified medical personnel consider treatment necessary and perform the treatment. This authorization is granted only if I cannot be reached and reasonable effort has been made to do so.

Parent or guardian: _____

Address: _____

Phone: (   ) _____ Other phone: (   ) _____

Additional contact in case of emergency: _____

Relationship to athlete: _____ Phone: (   ) _____

Family physician: _____ Phone: (   ) _____

Medical conditions (e.g., allergies, chronic illness): _____

_____

_____

_____

_____

My child and I are aware that participating in _____ is a potentially hazardous activity. We assume all risks associated with participation in this sport, including but not limited to falls, contact with other participants, and other reasonable-risk conditions associated with the sport. All such risks to my child are known and appreciated by my child and me.

We understand this informed consent form and agree to its conditions.

Athlete's signature: _____ Date: _____

Parent's or guardian's signature: _____

Date: _____

From ASEP, 2008, *Coaching youth track & field* (Champaign, IL: Human Kinetics).

Injury Report Form

Date of injury: _____ Time: _____ a.m./p.m.
Location: _____

Athlete's name: _____
Age: _____ Date of birth: _____

Type of injury: _____
Anatomical area involved: _____
Cause of injury: _____
_____
_____
_____

Extent of injury: _____
_____
_____
_____

Person administering first aid (name): _____
First aid administered: _____
_____
_____

Other treatment administered: _____
_____
_____

Referral action: _____
_____
_____
_____
_____

Signature of person administering first aid: _____
Date: _____

From ASEP, 2008, *Coaching youth track & field* (Champaign, IL: Human Kinetics).

Emergency Information Card

Athlete's name: _____ Date of birth: _____
Address: _____
Phone: (   ) _____

Contact Information
Parent's or guardian's name: _____
Address: _____
Phone: (   ) _____ Other phone: (   ) _____

Additional contact's name: _____
Relationship to athlete: _____
Address: _____
Phone: (   ) _____ Other phone: (   ) _____

Insurance Information
Name of insurance company: _____
Policy name and number: _____

Medical Information
Physician's name: _____
Phone: (   ) _____

Is your child allergic to any drugs?   *YES   NO*
If so, what? _____
Does your child have other allergies (e.g., bee stings, dust)? _____
_____

Does your child have any of the following?   *asthma   diabetes   epilepsy*
Is your child currently taking medication?   *YES   NO*
If so, what? _____

Does your child wear contact lenses?   *YES   NO*

Is there additional information we should know about your child's health or
physical condition?   *YES   NO*
If yes, please explain: _____
_____

Parent's or guardian's signature: _____
Date: _____

From ASEP, 2008, *Coaching youth track & field* (Champaign, IL: Human Kinetics).

Emergency Response Card

Be prepared to give the following information to an EMS dispatcher.
(*Note*: Do not hang up first. Let the EMS dispatcher hang up first.)

Caller's name: _____

Telephone number from which the call is being made: _____

Reason for call: _____

How many people are injured: _____

Condition of victim(s): _____

First aid being given: _____

Location: _____

Address: _____

City: _____

Directions (e.g., cross streets, landmarks, entrance access):

Appendix B

Track and Field Terms

This glossary of track and field terminology will help youth coaches become more familiar with some of the technical language used in the sport.

acceleration zone—A 10-meter area before the exchange zone used in relays. Outgoing runners may use this area to build up speed. (Acceleration zones are not used in the Hershey program.)

alternate action—The coordination of the arms and the legs in walking or running (for example, when the left arm goes forward, the left leg goes backward, and so on).

anaerobic—A term used to describe a muscular contraction that occurs without oxygen.

ancillary training—Any type of training that is not specific to the competitive task. This training is essential in preventing overspecialization and preventing athletes from focusing on event-specific training too early. Ancillary training can be used to develop posture, joint stability, endurance, and other attributes.

angle of release—In the throws, this angle measures the relationship between the implement and the ground during the first few feet of flight.

ATP—Adenosine triphosphate. The fuel that is consumed to produce muscular contraction.

back layout—A high jump technique in which athletes face away from the bar during clearance. Also known as the *Fosbury flop*.

backside mechanics—The leg and arm action that happens behind the center of mass during running.

bilateral training—Training both the left and right side of the body in order to provide some challenge for the nondominant side (for example, a right-handed thrower may use the left arm for some practice throws).

biomechanics—Using the laws of physics to understand principles of human movement.

block clearance—The initial two or three steps out of the starting blocks.

blocking—Bracing one part of the body to cause a transfer of momentum into the nonstopped parts. For example, a right-handed thrower would brace the left side of the body to allow the right side to whip around and accelerate the implement.

bounding—Locomotive jumping moves that look like exaggerated running.

braking—Casting out the lower leg during running in an attempt to lengthen the stride. This is not recommended because casting the leg out is like putting on the brakes.

breaking at the hips—Bending over at the waist while running (often occurs during fatigue). Breaking at the hips is dangerous because it elongates the hamstring and makes athletes more prone to injury.

center of mass (COM)—The average position of a body's matter, generally in the middle of the body. Note: The COM is not a fixed location. For example, an athlete's center of mass is raised when the arms go up, and it shifts forward when an athlete bends at the waist.

centrifugal force—A force that causes an object to move away from the center. Imagine getting smashed against the wall of an amusement park ride or how water is forced out of clothes during the spin cycle.

concentric contraction—The shortening of a muscle to cause movement in a joint.

connective tissue—The sinews (tendons, ligaments, and cartilage).

conservation of angular momentum—The biomechanical principle that describes how a short lever moves faster than a long lever. Runners can take advantage of this principle by shortening the back leg as it swings forward during the running stroke.

core strength—The ability of the muscles of the trunk and hips to control posture and produce force.

cross steps—The final steps in an athlete's approach before throwing the javelin. During the cross steps, the implement is withdrawn, and the athlete uses an aggressive forward swing of the back leg. For children throwing the minijavelin or softball, this move resembles the crow hop that an outfielder would use in baseball.

crouch start—The loaded athletic position used at the beginning of races when athletes are not using blocks.

density—The ratio of work to rest during a training session.

dorsiflex—Preflexing the foot so that the ankle is at a right angle.

dynamic—With some speed, looseness, and range of motion.

eccentric contraction—The lengthening of a muscle to allow movement in a joint.

elasticity—The ability to recruit the connective tissues to create more economical movement.

endurance—The ability to expend energy over time.

exchange zone—A 20-meter area marked on the track that designates where the baton may be legally passed during a relay race.

extensive tempo—A type of running workout characterized by submaximal effort (generally less than 80 percent of maximum effort). The focus is usually on technique, rhythm, and getting in some volume.

false start—Initiating movement in a race before the starter's signal.

fartlek—A type of workout that involves running at various speeds. *Fartlek* is a Swedish word meaning "speed play."

fly zone—A measured area (usually 30 meters or less) used to time full-speed running; acceleration is not considered. The acceleration zone (10 meters before the exchange zone) used in USATF is also sometimes called a fly zone.

focal point—A point that athletes focus their eyes on as part of their technique. For example, shot-putters keep their eyes on a focal point directly behind the ring (about 10-15 feet back). This helps the athletes maintain shoulder–hip separation as they land in the power position.

foul—The result recorded by officials in the field events when athletes do not execute legal attempts. Sometimes called a *scratch*.

general strength—The ability to move one's own weight. For example, this type of strength is demonstrated by doing push-ups, sit-ups, body weight squats, and lunges.

go-mark—A mark that outgoing runners in a relay race may place on the track (usually marked with a piece of tape) to indicate when they should begin running. The outgoing runner begins accelerating when the incoming runner reaches the go-mark.

grip height—The height of the athlete's top hand on the pole (measured to the end of the pole) when performing the pole vault.

ground contact time—The amount of time each foot contact takes during running. As athletes fatigue, ground contact time increases.

hammer—The implement that athletes throw for distance in the hammer throw event. This implement consists of a heavy ball attached to the end of a wire.

heat—A preliminary race.

heel recovery—Bending at the knee to bring the leg forward during the recovery phase of running.

heel–toe relationship—Refers to the proper placement of the feet when an athlete is in the power position for the throwing events. In this position, the toe of the front foot is aligned with the heel of the back foot. This alignment allows the hips to rotate completely through.

hinged moment—The sudden creation of a point of rotation that causes a transfer of momentum (see blocking).

impact area—The designated area for the implements to land in a throwing event.

intensity—The measure of effort in training or competition.

intensive tempo—A type of running workout characterized by near maximal effort (generally more than 90 percent of maximum effort). The focus is typically on running at race pace and developing the ability to run fast when tired (maintaining technique and fast ground contact time).

interval—A type of workout with predetermined rest periods between bouts of running. Usually, the rest intervals are short (one to three minutes), and the athlete begins the next effort before recovering completely from the previous one.

kick—A final burst of speed in a distance event.

lifting—A violation in the race walk characterized by both feet being noticeably off the ground.

maximum controllable speed—In the jumps, this is the most speed an athlete can develop on the runway while still being able to effectively jump.

maximum velocity mechanics—Refers to the technique that sprinters should use when they have reached full speed in a race (after the acceleration phase).

overspeed—A developmentally advanced training technique in which some type of assistance is used (such as bungee cords, pulley systems, or slight declines) to allow the athlete to run slightly faster than full speed.

overstride—Artificially lengthening the running stride by casting the lower leg out. Overstriding causes longer ground contact times, leads to a braking action, and puts tremendous pressure on the already stressed posterior chain.

overuse—A term used to describe injuries or chronic fatigue caused by too much training and competition.

parabolic curve—The path of a nonaerodynamic object in flight.

penultimate step—The next-to-last foot contact during a jumper's approach run.

physiology—The study of the body's systems and parts.

plantarflex—An improper technique in track and field that involves pointing the toe away from the knee.

plateau—A point in training where an athlete no longer demonstrates improvement.

posterior chain—The muscles of the back of the body (gastrocnemius, hamstrings, gluteus).

progressive loading—Gradually adding volume or intensity to a training program over the course of the season.

race modeling—A type of workout that consists of rehearsing specific parts of a race.

range throwing—Throwing workouts designed with an inverse relationship of volume to intensity.

recovery phase—The phase of the running stroke in which the leg is swinging forward in the air (the foot is not in contact with the track).

resisted runs—Running up hills or while towing an object (such as a sled or tire).

rest—The recovery or regeneration period when training.

retrieval—Collecting implements (shots, discuses, and so forth) from the impact area after a round of throwing.

rhythm endurance—The ability to maintain rhythm over time, especially in a state of fatigue.

runway—A designated area or lane where jumpers perform their approach run to build up speed before leaping.

scissors jump—A high jump technique in which athletes jump off of their outside foot and lift the inside leg over the crossbar, followed by the jumping leg. The leg action looks like scissors opening and closing as the athlete clears the bar.

set position—The still position that runners must assume immediately before the starting command.

shot put—A field event in which athletes push a heavy ball directly from the shoulder area with the goal of making the ball travel as far as possible.

shoulder–hip separation—The position of the hips and shoulders (hips open, shoulders closed) that results from the rotation of the spine when an athlete is in the power position for the throws. This twisting of the trunk recruits the abdominal muscles for the throwing action.

specificity—Using training activities that are very similar to the competitive task.

speed endurance—The ability to run at high intensities over distance.

speed work—High-quality training that involves short repetitions of full-speed running.

sprint—A short race run at full speed in lanes.

stabilizers—The small muscles that stabilize a joint.

standards—The adjustable uprights that support the crossbar in the high jump or pole vault. This term is also used to refer to the qualifying marks needed to enter invitational or championship meets.

starting blocks—Adjustable metal pedals that athletes use as a pushing surface for the first movement in sprint races.

static—Holding still (the opposite of dynamic).

steeplechase—A distance race in which athletes must clear four heavy barriers and a water jump on each lap. This event is part of the Junior Olympics program.

stimulus—In training theory, this word is used to describe the type and quantity of activity.

stretch reflex—The immediate contraction of a muscle following a stretch.

stride frequency—The rate of turnover in the running stride. Also called *stride rate*.

summate force—The cumulative force generated by a series of contractions of different muscles.

summation of forces—The biomechanical principle that calls for using the larger muscles first to build momentum, followed by the smaller, faster muscles toward the end of a movement.

surge—A brief burst of acceleration during a distance race.

toe board—A raised wooden or fiberglass part of the shot put circle.

torque—Force generated by rotation about an axis. In the throws, shoulder–hip separation is the key to producing torque.

triple jump—A field event consisting of three phases (a "hop, step, and jump") measured collectively for distance.

variability—Using different workouts and training ideas to keep children interested and to provide a well-rounded program.

volume—The overall amount of work done during a training session or cycle (week, month, or season).

About ASEP

Coaching Youth Track & Field was written by the American Sport Education Program (ASEP) in conjunction with Matt Lydum and other experts from Hershey's Track & Field Games and USA Track & Field.

Matt Lydum is actively involved in the sport of track and field at the national and international levels. He has served as USOC delegate to the International Olympic Academy and on the USA coaching staff for the World Championships in Youth Athletics. As a coaching educator, he has certified hundreds of high school coaches in the Great Lakes region and around the country and coordinates the Instructor Training Course for USA Track & Field.

USA Track & Field (USATF) is the national governing body for track and field, long-distance running, and race walking in the United States. USATF encompasses the world's oldest organized sports, the most-watched events of Olympic broadcasts, the number-one high school and junior high school participatory sport, and more than 30 million adult runners in the United States. Nearly 100,000 Americans are members of USATF. The mission of USATF is to foster sustained competitive excellence, interest, and participation in the sports of track and field, long-distance running, and race walking.

Hershey's Track & Field program promotes youth physical fitness and is the largest program of its kind in the United States and Canada with more than 400,000 participants. Hershey's Track & Field Games encourage children ages 14 and under to participate in track and field events. Regardless of a child's ability, each child is treated like a winner.

ASEP has been developing and delivering coaching education courses since 1981. As the nation's leading coaching education program, ASEP works with national, state, and local youth sport organizations to develop educational programs for coaches, officials, administrators, and parents. These programs incorporate ASEP's philosophy of "Athletes first, winning second."